SOUTHERN BAPTIST SISTERS

BAPTISTS

HISTORY, LITERATURE, THEOLOGY, HYMNS

General Editor: Walter B. Shurden is the Callaway Professor of Christianity in the Roberts Department of Christianity and Executive Director of the Center for Baptist Studies, Mercer University, Macon, Georgia.

John Taylor, *Baptists on the American Frontier: A History of Ten Baptist Churches*
Edited by Chester Young
Thomas Helwys, *A Short Declaration of the Mystery of Iniquity*
Edited by Richard Groves
Roger Williams, The Bloody Tenant of Persecution for Cause of Conscience
Edited by Richard Groves
Edwin Gaustad, Historical Introduction
James A. Rogers†, *Richard Furman: Life and Legacy*
Lottie Moon, *Send the Light: Lottie Moon's Letters and Other Writings*
Edited by Keith Harper
James Byrd, *The Challenges of Roger Williams: Religious Liberty, Violent Persecution, and the Bible*
Anne Dutton, *The Influential Spiritual Writings of Anne Dutton: Volume 1: Letters*
Edited by JoAnn Ford Watson (Fall 2003)
David T. Morgan, *Southern Baptist Sisters: In Search of Status, 1845-2000* (Fall 2003)
William E. Ellis, *"A Man of Books and a Man of the People":*
E. Y. Mullins and the Crisis of Moderate Southern Baptist Leadership (Fall 2003)
Jarrett Burch, *Adiel Sherwood: Baptist Antebellum Pioneer in Georgia* (Winter 2003)
Anthony Chute, *A Piety Above the Common Standard: Jesse Mercer and the Defense of Evangelistic Calvinism* (Spring 2004)

SOUTHERN BAPTIST SISTERS

In Search of Status, 1845–2000

BY

DAVID T. MORGAN

Mercer University Press
Macon, Georgia
MMIII

ISBN 0-86554-830-7
MUP/P273

First Edition.

Library of Congress Cataloging-in-Publication Data

Morgan, David T.
 Southern Baptist sisters : in search of status, 1845-2000 / c by David
T. Morgan.— 1st ed.
    p. cm.
Includes bibliographical references and index.
 ISBN 0-86554-830-7 (hardcover : alk. paper)
1. Southern Baptist Convention—History. 2. Baptist women—Southern
States—History. 3. Sex role—Religious aspects—Baptists—History. I. Title.
 BX6207.S68M67 2003
 286'.132'082--dc22

                                                                2003016082

CONTENTS

In memory of my mother, Bessie Herring Morgan, a lifelong Southern Baptist, who always encouraged me to work hard and strive for excellence.

ACKNOWLEDGMENTS

The writer is indebted to a number of people for their assistance in the research and writing of this work. The logical place for me to initiate my research was at the Southern Baptist Historical Library and Archives in Nashville, Tennessee, a rich depository that I have visited many times, and once again my friend Bill Sumners, the archivist there, was most accommodating. As in the past, I made numerous visits to the Special Collections at the Samford University Library, where Elizabeth Wells and her staff were helpful as always. Research for this work took me for the first time to the excellent library of the Woman's Missionary Union at the WMU headquarters building in Birmingham, Alabama. Heather Watters, librarian, and Betsy Lowery, archivist, provided kind and highly useful assistance. I thank all of these wonderful people for the help they so willingly gave.

I am also deeply indebted to some outstanding women for agreeing to give me interviews that, in my opinion, enriched the work enormously. They are: Denise Jacks and Dr. Shirley Richards, who minister as hospital chaplains in Birmingham; Sarah Jackson Shelton, who at the time of the interview was serving as interim minister of Baptist Church of the Covenant in Birmingham; and Wanda Lee, executive director Woman's Missionary Union. All of them were most cordial and offered insightful comments regarding women and their role in the Southern Baptist Convention. I sincerely thank them all.

No matter how many times one proofreads what one has written, one will invariably overlook mistakes that another's eyes will detect. Being fully aware of this, I persuaded my former student and colleague,

Professor Ruth Truss of the University of Montevallo, to read the manuscript. Professor Truss, an experienced and superb copyeditor, found far more mistakes than I ever dreamed I had made. Thus, my former student gave me an appreciated lesson in copyediting, and I am most grateful to her for it.

My wife Judy and many other well-wishers offered encouragement during the time that I was writing the book. Among the well-wishers were Professor Randall Miller of St. Joseph's University and Dr. Marc Jolley of Mercer University Press. I sincerely thank all of those who encouraged me along the way and expressed an interest in my completing the work.

PREFACE

Southern Baptist women played no part in the founding of the Southern Baptist Convention. They have, however, played a vital part in its growth and development, helping to make it the largest Protestant denomination in the United States. One would never know it, however, by reading the various histories of the SBC. More than one Baptist historian has pointed out that Southern Baptist women have been insultingly glossed over in histories of the convention, being mentioned only intermittently in tomes that run to hundreds of pages. That they have not been given their due is painfully obvious. They are not unique in being ignored and neglected. The same has been the lot of women in other mainline religious denominations; women in Episcopal, Lutheran, Methodist, and Presbyterian churches have fared little, if any, better. In the Roman Catholic Church, male chauvinism is entrenched as solidly, if not more solidly, than it is in the Protestant denominations. What must be noted, however, is that in the last half of the twentieth century a preponderance of mainline Protestant churches began to see the injustice of denying women a place equal to men, while Southern Baptists, especially in the final quarter of the century, joined the Roman Catholics and the Church of Jesus Christ of Latter Day Saints in holding fast to policies that ensure male domination of their respective organizations.

In spite of the subjugation of Southern Baptist women, they have produced from their ranks some strong leaders, and a few of them have made it clear that they have chafed under their subordinate status. Yet, even those impressive women have been unusually patient and have refrained from asserting their right to equal status. They and those who follow them have been content to do what they believe God has called them to do, mainly working through the Woman's Missionary Union, which they founded in 1888, and by going out as missionaries both at home and abroad. To avoid having Southern Baptist men dictate to them as they went about their work for foreign and home missions, the women had the foresight to make it clear that their organization was "auxiliary" to the Southern Baptist Convention and not a regular agency that might be subject to control by SBC male leaders. In the last quarter of the twentieth century women were placed under heavy pressure by fundamentalist leaders of the Convention who sought to dictate the WMU's agenda in the same way they dictated the agendas of the various denominational agencies. The word "auxiliary" proved a godsend to the WMU in their struggle not to knuckle under to these pressures. They resisted the pressure so successfully that the fundamentalist leaders were forced to begin organizing an alternative organization for Southern Baptist women.

For decades the WMU exerted a mighty effort on behalf of Southern Baptist missions, but the women of that organization did not receive due credit. Nor did other Southern Baptist women outside of the WMU who contributed to the convention's work win adequate recognition and appreciation. No doubt Southern Baptist sisters felt that Southern Baptist men in general and denominational leaders in particular were lacking in gratitude. No one seemed to care what part the women might want to play in the Convention's affairs. The role they would play was decided for them by their husbands and other Southern Baptist brethren. Amazingly, it was not until the 1970s that a significant number of Southern Baptist women decided that it was time to assert themselves by seeking leadership roles in their denomination and by insisting on the right of women to be ordained to the ministry and to serve as pastors of churches. It was not until 1983 that they formed an organization called Southern Baptist Women in Ministry to support and promote their cause. In reaction to this assertiveness, fundamentalist leaders secured passage of resolutions aimed at keeping women in their place. At Kansas City in 1984 such a resolution encouraged the service of women "in all aspects of church life and work other than pastoral functions and leadership roles entailing ordination." The dubious rationale for the resolution was that man was created first, while woman was first in "the Edenic fall." A follow-up resolution in 1998 called upon women to be submissive to their husbands, and another in 2000 excluded women from ordination for the pastoral ministry. The inequality that Southern Baptist women have suffered was brought about mainly by men ignoring them or simply reminding them that the Bible clearly says that women should keep silent in the churches. When that would no longer work, the fundamentalist leaders, who had fought for and gained control of the Southern Baptist Convention during the 1980s, institutionalized women's subordination with the formal and forthright resolutions noted above. Thus, Southern Baptist women have been subordinate to men since the Convention's founding, and that subordination continues right up to the minute that these words are being written. As long as fundamentalists remain in control of the SBC, the "women-must-be-submissive" policy will stay in place.

INTRODUCTION

It is a great irony that the consistently male-dominated Southern Baptist Convention cannot point to a man in its history as "the" exemplary denominational figure about whom nearly every other Southern Baptist has heard. There was a time when *most* Southern Baptists knew who George W. Truett was, but today only the older generation of Southern Baptists would remember this outstanding pastor of the First Baptist Church of Dallas, Texas. Truett was a prince among preachers in the early decades of the twentieth century. Another man who served First Baptist of Dallas for many years was W. A. Criswell, and he was widely known for decades after World War II. Both of these men enjoyed a large measure of fame from serving as pastor of one of the denomination's largest churches and from being in leadership roles in the SBC, but neither was as famous as the evangelist Billy Graham, another Southern Baptist but one who is usually identified as part of the worldwide Christian community. Many Southern Baptists are probably not aware that Graham is a part of their denomination, since the evangelist seldom mentions it. No, if Southern Baptists want to designate someone about whom nearly every Southern Baptist has heard, they must single out a woman, a woman small of stature who served as a missionary to China for forty years. Her name was Charlotte Digges Moon, known to nearly every Southern Baptist as Lottie Moon. The dedication of this woman in spreading the Christian gospel to the

Chinese for so many years resulted in the Woman's Missionary Union's institutionalizing an annual offering for foreign missions on her recommendation. When Lottie Moon proposed that such an offering be taken each year, she did not dream that the offering would be named for her. That offering has raised countless millions of dollars to support Southern Baptist mission work around the world. For over a century Southern Baptists have been asked every year to contribute to the Christmas offering that would ultimately be called the Lottie Moon Christmas Offering. Only one other Southern Baptist, another woman, has her name mentioned annually in all Southern Baptist churches: Annie Armstrong, one of the founders of the WMU and the woman for whom an offering is taken every Easter for home missions, but that offering did not bear Armstrong's name until 1934.

Thus, promoting foreign and home missions, a large part of what Southern Baptists claim they exist to do, has been carried out for many years by using the names of two remarkable Southern Baptist women. This is not to say, of course, that men have not contributed to the promotion of missionary activity, for many Southern Baptist men have given their lives as missionaries on various mission fields. However, the most outstanding missionary ever to go out under the SBC banner was a woman, Lottie Moon, and probably the most fervent spirit among Southern Baptists in promoting mission work both at home and abroad was another woman, Annie Armstrong. Justifiably, they are the most famous Southern Baptists and probably always will be, in spite of all that the current fundamentalist leadership in the SBC can do to deny women equality with men in that denomination.

Denied equal status, women nevertheless continued to contribute to the denomination in many ways other than serving as missionaries and carrying on mission work through the WMU. They were quite active in Sunday school work, tending to dominate it, thus causing some ministers to have serious doubts about the value of Sunday school. Some leaders accepted women working in Sunday school as long as they did not teach men or mixed classes. Women also came to play a role in theological education. Since so many of them went to the mission fields and had seminary training before going, they gradually gained greater visibility as trained and dedicated servants of God and won some recognition for their contributions.

While the involvement of women in Southern Baptist activities continued to grow, there was little inclination on the part of male leaders to give them equal status in denominational affairs. Finally, the women decided that enough was enough. Since 1978 some Southern Baptist women have made it clear that they will not quietly submit any longer to being treated as second-class members of the SBC. On 22 September of that year the first national meeting of Southern Baptist women was held by them to consider their opportunities and the obstacles they faced as they sought to minister. Held in Nashville, the meeting was called the Consultation on Women in Church-Related Vocations. Gladys S. Lewis, a former missionary under the auspices of the SBC's Foreign Mission Board, delivered a stirring keynote address titled "Awake, Deborah, Arise." Lewis was not ordained and did not seek ordination, but she considered herself a minister and urged women to work out their ministry as best they could in relation to the SBC. Among those in attendance were several ordained women and some prominent Southern Baptists of both sexes from the ranks of academia. Catherine B. Allen of the WMU chaired the meeting. Lynda Williams-Weaver, a woman pastor from Kentucky; Sue Fitzgerald, also an ordained Southern Baptist minister; Professor Sarah Frances Anders of Louisiana College; Professor Frank Stagg and his wife Evelyn of Southern Baptist Seminary; and Milton Ferguson, Randall Lolley, and Roy Honeycutt, presidents respectively of Midwestern, Southeastern, and Southern seminaries were all present. Jimmy Allen, a prominent Southern Baptist pastor and SBC president, was there too as a featured speaker.

Since that significant meeting in 1978 more Southern Baptist women have sought and gained ordination as deacons and pastors, even though most Southern Baptist churches have persisted in denying women ordination, especially as pastors. Now, the policy of denying women ordination as pastors has been institutionalized by the denomination, and Southern Baptist women in the year 2000 seemed to be right back where they started in 1845.

The truth of the matter is that the Southern Baptist Convention has produced some outstanding leaders of both sexes, but precious few women—Moon and Armstrong being only two of a handful of exceptions—have received any glory, and none have enjoyed any power. Although a couple of women have been elected as vice president of the SBC and some have served on the denomination's Executive Committee, those women were never taken seriously by most of the men who actually held the reins of authority. The following pages will demonstrate that there were some Southern Baptist men who abhorred the inequality that women suffered and made efforts to alter that policy, which, though usually unspoken and unofficial, was nonetheless firmly entrenched. Most of the brothers, however, were either indifferent or determined to maintain male domination.

This study will also show that men's attitude toward women during the history of the Southern Baptist Convention has fluctuated. At times the sisters have enjoyed more status than at other times. Almost invariably when women in American society won battles and made gains in status, similar gains were realized by women in the Southern Baptist Convention. For example, Southern Baptist men, along with many others, resisted woman's suffrage, but when women all over America pushed for the right to vote for national, state, and local political leaders, this led to Southern Baptist women gaining the right to go to the annual conventions as messengers and to cast their ballots to elect officers and decide denominational issues.

Unfortunately, when victories were won, they were often followed by periods when Southern Baptist men dug in their heels and became determined to prevent women from making further progress. The 1920s through the 1950s saw Southern Baptist women make minimal gains in status but none in acquiring power. That began to change when the Women's Liberation movement, which had its beginnings in the 1960s, gradually gave impetus to a liberalization of attitudes among Southern Baptist men on women's issues. Unhappily, the liberalizing trend was followed quickly by a conservative reaction in the 1970s. As a consequence, Southern Baptist fundamentalists rose to power in the denomination during the 1980s, and after 1984 the women of the SBC once again found themselves where their female ancestors had been when the denomination was founded in 1845. The denomination was founded for the purpose of affirming the Southern way of life—a way of life that featured a society dominated by white males, a society in which women were put on a pedestal and adored as long as they acquiesced in their subordinate position, and a society—worst of all—that held black people in slavery and regarded doing so as an act of Christian charity.

This book is not intended to be a complete history of women in the Southern Baptist Convention during the denomination's first century and a half. Although such a book needs to be written, producing such a study would be a long and arduous undertaking. The purpose here is far more modest; it is to explore a particular aspect of women in the Southern Baptist Convention—namely, their role in promoting the denomination's growth and development in the face of male fears that too much activity on the part of women would lead to their gaining control over the SBC. Southern Baptist men, like men of other denominations and American men in general, believed that women had a God-appointed position to occupy both in church and in society at large. In church they were to attend, to give, and to keep silent. In society they were to serve as homemakers and to be subservient to their husbands. While many men in most denominations have come to see the injustice in such an attitude and have moved toward equality for women in church affairs, that has not been true of most men in the Southern Baptist Convention. After more than a century and a half since the founding of the Southern Baptist Convention, Southern Baptist sisters are still in search of status!

CHAPTER 1

"NEAR THE CITY OF SODOM"

ATTITUDES OF SOUTHERN BAPTISTS AND OTHERS TOWARD WOMEN

In the early years of the twentieth century male chauvinist attitudes toward women were voiced among Southern Baptists nowhere more vociferously than in the *Western Recorder*, the journal sponsored by Kentucky Baptists. Reacting against women organizing clubs and demanding the right to vote, the editor of the *Recorder* claimed that "this masculine female tribe" was trying to "unsex and unchristianize" American women and warned that "once we have crossed the boundaries established by God's Word, we are already near the city of Sodom." Such a view was by no means peculiar to that editor or to Southern Baptists. It was merely a reflection of the attitude that prevailed in nearly all churches and in American society at the time—at least among the majority of males and particularly among fundamentalists and other biblical literalists. The idea, often labeled "Victorian," that God had ordained separate spheres for men and women was still widely accepted, and most men saw attempts by women to gain more rights as rebellion against both man and God.[1]

Even before the male-dominated society of the nineteenth century was designated "Victorian," women had already begun to chafe under their repression, and at Seneca Falls, New York, in 1848 they called for reforms aimed at giving women equality with men. Determined to maintain their dominance, men reasserted their authority, and in spite of a few victories, American women would wait more than a century for even a semblance of equal rights. The churches, including the Southern Baptist Convention, would be among the slowest to change. As recently as 1972, Georgia Harkness, a prominent female Methodist theologian, observed: "Thus it came about that a long-embedded paternalism, ecclesiastical restrictions, biblical literalism, Pauline prohibitions, and the pull of all of these in combination within the social structure denied to women for centuries their identity and equality as persons. In the nineteenth century the hard shell of custom began to crack." She noted further that "the church has lagged behind all the other principal social institutions in its admission of qualified women to leadership on terms of equality with men" and is the "last stronghold of male dominance."[2]

In one way Harkness's statement is misleading, for women have not been restricted to the same extent in all ages, at least not in the churches. There have even been times when women exercised leadership roles and worked in partnership with men, but such instances have been rare. The earliest Protestants, for example, were willing to have women serve as partners in spreading the gospel, and there was a number of women who were

---

[1] Betty A. DeBerg, *Ungodly Women: Gender and the First Wave of American Fundamentalism* (Macon: Mercer University Press, 2000; Fortress, 1990) 43, 45, 51; *Western Recorder*, 10 August 1911, 8.

[2] Georgia Harkness, *Women in Church and Society* (Nashville: Abingdon Press, 1972) 27, 85.

active in the Reformation. None of the Protestants, however, allowed women to preach, except Martin Luther, and even he did so only when no men were available. As a general rule, even the radical Anabaptists did not admit women to the pulpit, but there were exceptions. Women, as a rule, did not participate in choosing church officials. Even so, they did help to found Anabaptist churches and informally spread Anabaptist views. Occasionally Anabaptist women assumed leadership roles, as did the Dutch woman Elizabeth of Leeuwarden, among others.[3] Again, however, those instances were exceptions to the rule.

Whatever leeway women enjoyed as church leaders during the sixteenth century began to slip away in the seventeenth when ministers began to stress the fact that Eve was responsible for leading the human race into sin. The drift toward reducing women's participation had its perils in America, for women outnumbered men in most churches, sometimes by a significant margin. To alienate them would have been imprudent. Hence, Puritan ministers in New England in particular found it necessary to state their case very carefully. Though claiming that women, because of Eve's sin, were supposed to be subject to men and experience pain in childbirth, the usual line was that God had mercifully converted these curses of women into blessings by using their experiences to make them "tender" and pious and innately more religious than men.[4]

The feminization of American churches continued and became more pronounced by the turn of the eighteenth century. Women gained a striking visibility as their numbers grew ever larger, and they emerged as pillars of many Protestant churches in the evangelical community. The Great Awakening, led by George Whitefield, a maverick Anglican priest, shook all of the

---

[3] Richard L. Greaves, ed., *Triumph over Silence: Women in Protestant History* (Westport CT and London: Greenwood Press, 1985) 4–6, 51–53.

[4] Nancy F. Cott, *The Bonds of Womanhood* (New Haven: Yale University Press, 1977) 126–27, 146.

American colonies in 1740 and following. Other revivals had broken out during the two decades before Whitefield arrived in America, but they were less intense and widespread. It was Whitefield, whose greatest patron was a woman, the Countess of Huntingdon, who moved all of America as no one ever had before. Advocates of the Awakening encouraged women to take an active part in the work of God.[5]

Some new groups, like the Separate Baptists, who were the spiritual offspring of George Whitefield, allowed women to lead as well as to support. Women spoke at their public meetings, but Regular Baptists could not accept this, insisting that only ordained ministers should preach. Methodists at that juncture also allowed women more freedom to participate than some other churches did, and Quakers boldly proclaimed the spiritual equality of men and women.[6]

Historian Susan Juster contends that for most of the eighteenth century Baptist women shared power in governing the churches, participating along with men in selecting and firing ministers, admitting new members, and ejecting backsliding ones. However, this was true mainly in churches that supported the Great Awakening, was never true in conservative Congregational churches, and was abandoned by evangelical churches late in the century when the evangelical community sought to "distance itself from the 'disorderly' women who disrupted congregational life."[7]

Because of its radical nature and its transforming effect on society in general, the American Revolution should have

---

[5] Greaves, *Triumph over Silence*, 126; Susan Hill Lindley, *"You Have Stept Out of Your Place:" A History of Women and Religion in America* (Louisville: Westminster/John Knox Press, 1996) 47.

[6] Julia Cherry Spruill, *Women's Life and Work in the Southern Colonies* (Chapel Hill: University of North Carolina Press, 1938) 247–49.

[7] Susan Juster, *Sexual Politics and Evangelism in Revolutionary New England* (Ithaca: Cornell University Press, 1995) 2, 4–5.

liberated American women, at least to some extent. Such was not the case, however. The somewhat assertive Abigail Adams urged her husband John to remember the ladies when he helped form the government, but he did not. Nor did his fellow founders of the American Republic. Although women had emerged from their "circumscribed sphere" for a brief time during the heat of the struggle against Great Britain and were praised for their notable contributions, the Revolution had no permanent effect on the status of women. The prevailing view in post-Revolutionary America was that women should remain quietly at home. What was true for women in American society became true for women in the vast majority of churches. Although some women had influence, in general women were expected to be quiet onlookers. All groups tended to agree that women should have no voice in church affairs.[8]

According to Juster, the evangelical church "masculinized its polity and its mission" after the Revolution. Since women were not made citizens of the republic, they were no longer considered citizens of the churches. Instead they were dependents in "a household ruled by men."[9]

In the nineteenth century this attitude came to be institutionalized in law and custom, but such a development should hardly have come as a surprise, for women in general had never enjoyed any real power in church or state for an extended period. Still, there had been freer times for women in days gone by. While women continued to have an informal influence on church actions, they were usually not praised for their godliness and contributions until their funerals. Only on rare occasions were women allowed to speak in public. In every instance, women were expected to occupy a place subordinate to men. Reverend Oliver Rufus Blue, a Methodist minister from

---

[8] Spruill, *Women's Life and Work*, 244–46.
[9] Juster, *Disorderly Women*, 12.

Montgomery, Alabama, attended a women's rights convention in New York City in 1853 and was appalled at the speeches delivered by "notorious infidels, abolitionists, and bloomers." Women who attended that meeting should have been, according to Blue, at home "attending" to their children, and he judged Lucy Stone, a leading feminist organizer, to be "very little above a common strumpet."[10]

One of the main barriers to women making any advances toward equality in early America and indeed in the English-speaking world was the law, which was based on English common law and the statutes of the British Parliament. When it came to interpreting English law, no one loomed larger in the English-speaking world in the eighteenth and nineteenth centuries than Sir William Blackstone, the famous jurist and legal historian who died in 1780. Sir William apparently did not hold women in high esteem. He asserted that "the husband and wife are one, and that one is the husband." Marriage ended a woman's legal identity, for upon saying "I do" she ceased to have property rights, a right to the money she earned, the right to have custody of her children in case of divorce, and she could not testify in court or sit on a jury. Nor could she vote or attend a university, a law school, or a medical school. If a woman were abused by her husband or her father, there was no legal remedy for her. Sad to say, the churches supported this legal repression of women.[11]

Single women were another matter. Although there was a stigma attached to women remaining single and various societal pressures were used to push them into marriage, the single woman

---

[10] Wayne Flynt and Gerald Berkley, *Taking Christianity to China: Alabama Missionaries in the Middle Kingdom, 1850–1950* (Tuscaloosa and London: University of Alabama Press, 1997) 27; Christine Leigh Heyrman, *Southern Cross: The Beginnings of the Bible Belt* (New York: Alfred A. Knopf, 1997) 205.

[11] Barbara Goldsmith, *Other Powers: The Age of Suffrage, Spiritualism, and the Scandalous Victoria Woodhull* (New York: Alfred A. Knopf, 1998) 12–13.

was considered fully competent in legal matters. She could sue and be sued, make contracts, execute deeds, dispose of her estate through a will, and serve as a guardian of minors. Since most women caved in to the pressures to marry, the vast majority of them probably never knew what it was like to control property except when they became widows. When they married again, as most did, they lost all legal control over their lives once more.[12]

What was true of American women in all sections of the United States was doubly true in the South, where the community was obligated to enforce gender and family conventions. All ranks of Southern men agreed that women should be subordinate and perhaps even docile. The belief was virtually universal among Southern males that God had "appointed a place & a duty for females, *out of which* they can neither accomplish their destiny nor secure their happiness." Nearly all women were expected to marry and were under constant pressure to do so. When they did, of course, their legal existence was suspended, as they became "one" with their husbands, upon whom they were both dependent and subordinate.[13]

Besides the notion that women were made by God for marriage, women were encouraged to marry because there were few respectable jobs available to them. It was acceptable for women to work in the home as housekeepers, governesses, and teachers, but there was some doubt about women teaching school in the outside world.[14]

Although marriage meant dependency and perhaps security, it did not ordinarily mean an easy life. For, after the Southern woman assumed her prescribed role as wife and mother, she, in most cases, worked hard for the rest of her life, managing her household and having a baby every year or so. If she had doubts

---

[12] Spruill, *Women's Life and Work*, 340–41, 344, 346–47, 366.

[13] Bertram Wyatt-Brown, *Southern Honor: Ethics and Behavior in the Old South* (New York: Oxford University Press, 1982) 228, 254.

[14] Ibid., 228–30.

about the fairness of her situation, she usually kept them to herself. Those women who articulated their complaints regarding female status were, as a rule, quickly rebuked. Even so, there were those bold women who found it "shameful" that men had all the power. Some were even courageous enough to argue in favor of women speaking and praying in mixed church gatherings. Mary T. Gambrell of Meridian, Mississippi, writing in 1891 for the woman's journal called the *Baptist Basket,* scoffed at male preachers for "guarding the pulpit against the sacrilegious tread of feminine feet." Sallie Rochester Ford, a novelist and a writer for her husband's journal the *Christian Repository,* dared to preside over public sessions with men and women in attendance. Her husband, Samuel Howard Ford, a pastor in Louisville, Kentucky, as well as a publisher, supported his wife, but she came under vicious verbal attack for advocating that women should be permitted to pray and speak in meetings with men present.[15]

While there were a few extraordinary women who were not intimidated by men or society's pressures to conform to the image of the Southern lady, a preponderance of Southern women tried to do exactly what was expected of them. It was hard not to do so, for churches, schools, parents, books, and magazines delivered the same message: if a woman wanted to be loved, respected, and supported, she must be a lady. To defy the pattern and be unladylike would lead to a woman's becoming an outcast. No doubt many Southern women harbored secret thoughts that were in disagreement with their prescribed place, but religion consistently confirmed what society told them—and that was

---

[15] Catherine B. Allen, *Laborers Together with God: 22 Great Women in Baptist Life* (Birmingham AL: Woman's Missionary Union, 1987) 231–34; Elizabeth Fox-Genovese, *Within the Plantation Household: Black and White Women of the Old South* (Chapel Hill: University of North Carolina Press, 1988) 242, 247; Leon McBeth, "The Role of Women in Southern Baptist History," *Baptist History & Heritage* (January 1977): 11; Anne Firor Scott, *The Southern Lady: From Pedestal to Politics, 1830–1930* (Chicago and London: University of Chicago Press, 1970) 22–35, 44.

that they were inferior to men. Even evangelical churches, which had encouraged women in the eighteenth century to step out and be spiritually active, took a sexist turn in the nineteenth by reinforcing the image of the submissive woman.[16]

Although the idea that women should not venture from their proper sphere was deeply embedded in American and, especially, Southern society by the middle of the nineteenth century, forces were soon at work that would lead ultimately to a more liberal perspective. The Seneca Falls Convention of 1848, which launched the women's movement in America, has already been mentioned. The terrible Civil War, which shook the nation from 1861 to 1865, was another undermining, but subtle, force for change. During the war Southern women assumed responsibility for maintaining the food supply, producing cotton and wool for clothing, and providing for many other needs of soldiers in the field. They were praised for their contributions to the cause. In the decades following the Civil War and Reconstruction, Southern women moved beyond their traditional roles, doing work that was previously forbidden. Some got a taste of independence and found that they had a ready appetite for it.[17]

As women began to show signs of asserting themselves, Southern Baptist men in particular drew back in horror and then lashed out. Tandy Dix, a layman and a physician, argued that the welfare of the human race depended upon "the maintenance and cultivation of effeminacy in the female." He claimed that he wanted to save some "silly woman" who might place "herself before the public." Insisting that women were biologically and psychologically inferior to men, Dix said that they should be restricted to "the care of the husband, children, the easel, the piano, and the needle." Reflecting a similar sentiment eleven years later in 1895, another Baptist brother asserted in the.

---

[16] Scott, *The Southern Lady*, 5–9, 13, 17, 20–21.

[17] Ibid., 82, 102, 133.

Christian Index, the journal of Georgia Baptists, "Our hope lies in woman the saint, not in woman the amazon."[18]

That same year, 1895, an article appeared in the *Alabama Baptist* that likened assertive women to the prophet Isaiah's "daughters of Zion" who were "haughty, and walk with stretched forth necks and wanton eyes, walking and mincing as they go, and making a tinkling with their feet." A Baptist pastor named H. C. Hurley of Jasper, Alabama, wrote a twenty-five-page pamphlet that argued that women should stay home and keep quiet.[19]

Though men were willing to give women no authority, they gladly took the money women raised for home and foreign missions through sewing circles and "mite societies." Long before there was a Southern Baptist Convention, Baptist women and women of other denominations had worked diligently to promote both home and foreign missions. Indeed, it was chiefly women who enlisted the forces of the church in the mission enterprise, educating and marshaling the lay forces far more successfully than the mission boards of the various denominations had been able to do. Gradually the number of women missionaries surpassed that of men among Protestants. In 1830 women had made up 49 percent of the missionary force; in 1880 the number climbed to 57 percent; and by 1929 two-thirds of all Protestant missionaries in the field were women. All of this was brought about by women forming their own missionary societies, a step that men in all denominations viewed as a threat to their control. Hence the men worked to place the societies under control of the denominational missionary boards or to have the boards absorb them. In 1888 the Centenary Conference of Protestant Missions warned, "Woman's work in the foreign field must be careful to recognize the headship of man in ordering the affairs of the

---

[18] *The Christian Index* (28 May 1895) 8; McBeth, "The Role of Women in Southern Baptist History," 10.

[19] Flynt and Berkley, *Taking Christianity to China*, 28.

Kingdom of God.... 'Adam was first formed, then Eve,' and 'the head of the woman is the man.' This order of creation has not been changed by Redemption, and we must conform all our plans and policies for the uplifting of the race through the Power of the Gospel to the Divine ordinance."[20]

As women became more visible in missionary efforts and were clearly taking the lead away from the denominational boards, each denomination found it necessary to come to grips with these new developments. Presbyterians agonized over the "woman question" after 1870 because the women were increasingly active and their contributions were important to the progress of the denomination. While concessions were gradually made, it would still be eighty-six years before the Presbyterian Church USA ordained a woman to the ministry. The Methodists were forced to confront the "woman question" as well, when Anna Howard Shaw, an advocate of woman's suffrage, received a preacher's license in her home state of Michigan in 1873. Five years later she graduated from Boston University's School of Theology. The Methodist Episcopal Church refused to ordain her, and she left the church. In 1880, despite some opposition, she was ordained by the Methodist Protestant Church, New York Conference.[21] Such concessions to assertive women were infinitesimal in number, however, as most denominations agonized, made a concession or two, and remained basically

---

[20] R. Pierce Beaver, *American Protestant Women in World Mission: A History of the First Feminist Movement in North America* (Grand Rapids MI: William B. Eerdman's Publishing Co., 1968) 108, 111, 115, 179, 204; Fannie E. S. Heck, *In Royal Service: The Mission Work of Southern Baptist Women* (Richmond: Foreign Mission Board, 1913) 40–57, 173; Patricia R. Hill, *The World Their Household: The American Woman's Foreign Mission Movement and Cultural Transformation, 1870–1920* (Ann Arbor: University of Michigan Press, 1985) 2–3; Rufus Spain, *At Ease in Zion: A Social History of Southern Baptists, 1865–1900* (Nashville: Vanderbilt University Press, 1961) 170.

[21] Greaves, *Triumph over Silence*, 164–65, 203–18, 220.

reactionary. This was especially true of the Southern Baptist Convention.

In the very month that Southern Baptist women organized their Woman's Missionary Union, John A. Broadus, perhaps the foremost theologian among Southern Baptists at that juncture, made a statement opposing women speaking in public and taking a leadership role in the church. Like others, he apparently feared that a woman's missionary organization would lead to women mounting pulpits to preach. In trying to keep Virginia women out of the WMU, the Baptist General Association of Virginia declared, "We further fear that such an independent organization of women naturally tends toward a violation of the divine interdict against a woman's becoming a public religious teacher and leader—a speaker before mixed assemblies, a platform declaimer, a pulpit proclaimer, street preacher, lyceum lecturer, stump orator." Another Baptist voice proclaimed, "The only four things any Christian can do for missions are to pray, to give, to talk, to go.... Three of these are open to women.... They may give and pray and go to their heart's content."[22] But please, ladies, no talking!

Obviously the prospect of women speaking to mixed audiences and presiding over meetings seriously disturbed conservative men—especially Southern Baptists. Presbyterians were nearly as bad, however, as a majority of that church's presbyteries opposed women organizing for mission activities beyond the local church. Not until 1904 were Presbyterian women allowed to organize their Woman's Auxiliary. The Woman's Foreign Missionary Society of the Methodist Protestant Church, which was organized in 1879, lost its independence when the general conference of that church forced it by constitutional revision to become a servant of the

---

[22] Quotes from the *Baltimore Baptist* and the *Western Recorder* in Catherine B. Allen, *A Century to Celebrate: History of Woman's Missionary Union* (Birmingham AL: Woman's Missionary Union, 1987) 13, 31.

denomination's board of foreign missions. In most denominations the story was nearly the same—women's groups created to further the cause of missions became either subordinate to or auxiliary to the denominational boards.[23]

Not only were the mainline Protestant denominations troubled by women organizing on a national scale and taking the lead in mission work at home and abroad, they had difficulty deciding on the acceptability of women missionaries. All of them favored sending married women along with their husbands, and all of them regarded the husband as the missionary and the wife as a helper. The problem was single women who offered themselves as missionaries in increasing numbers. This was a real concern, for as restricted as women were in the United States, it was far worse for them in mission fields such as China, India, and Burma, where women had no rights and were treated as servants. From the 1830s on there were a few single women missionaries sent out, some from various denominations, but as of 1861 there was only one unmarried woman missionary left, a "Miss Marston," who served in Burma. That picture changed over the next several decades with the organization after the Civil War of the various women's missionary boards and societies. By 1900 there were 41 women's boards of foreign missions in the United States, and by 1909 there were 4,710 unmarried women on foreign mission fields, nearly 2,000 of them from the United States.[24] Thus, in spite of all the opposition women faced from their husbands, their brothers, and their fathers who ran the denominational mission boards, they persisted and followed their desires to go themselves or to send their sisters, single as well as married, to the mission fields of the world. They would not be denied.

---

[23] Beaver, *American Protestant Women in World Mission*, 53, 61–63, 103–107: Hill, *The World Their Household*, 53.

[24] Beaver, *American Protestant Women in World Mission*, 71–86, 88; Helen Barrett Montgomery, *Western Women in Eastern Lands* (New York: The Macmillan Co., 1910) 10, 19, 24, 243.

As the nineteenth century chugged along toward its end, women were removing at least a few barriers to equality. Since women's powerful interest in missions was one driving force behind their progress, it would seem that racism might have been set aside and that black and white women might have united as sisters. Such was not the case in the Southern United States. In fact, race was one reason Southern white women felt compelled to endure their subordinate position. Firmly entrenched in the culture of the now-Jim Crow South was the notion that white did not mix with black, and white women needed their husbands to protect them from black men. In Dixie it was white versus black, and women of the two races could never form a political base to work together against male domination.[25]

Although women—at least white women—had made some gains as legal beings by the 1890s, they were still a long way away from full equality with men. Four states—Wyoming, Utah, Colorado, and Idaho—allowed women to vote in state and federal elections. Some states gave wives control over their inherited property and earnings. In case of divorce, women could expect, in some states at least, to obtain joint custody of their children. Even so, in most states they could still not vote, hold office, or enter into a business partnership without the consent of their husbands.[26]

Women entered the twentieth century, despite a few legal gains, still laboring under the burden of male domination, and most men intended to keep it that way. To American men in general and Southern men in particular, a woman's place was still that of wife, mother, and homemaker. The vast majority of women in the twentieth century complied with what was

[25] Sheila M. Rothman, *Woman's Proper Place: A History of Changing Ideals and Practices, 1870 to the Present* (New York: Basic Books, 1978) xiv, 34.

[26] Lois W. Banner, *Women in Modern America: A Brief History* (New York: Harcourt, Brace, and Jovanovich, 1974) 2–3.

expected by marrying and becoming housewives and mothers. During the entire century, approximately 90 percent of American women were married at some time in their lives. Even though the movement for women's rights that dated back to the Seneca Falls Convention was still going strong and demanding suffrage for women, most Southern women were not caught up in it, and this greatly pleased some Southern ministers. At a ministers' meeting in Montgomery, Alabama, in 1900, the Reverend W. J. Elliott said, "It is gratifying to know that our Southern women are not seeking to rule in the church and state."[27]

With or without the assistance of Southern women, women in other parts of the nation were determined to secure the right to vote, believing firmly that this would lead to other freedoms. To some extent their hopes were fulfilled following the ratification of the Nineteenth Amendment in 1920. Many women got jobs and left home, living in their own apartments. By 1930 almost two million women were employed as secretaries, typists, and file clerks. Another 700,000 worked as salespersons in department stores. Most women so employed lived in cities. The economic results of this significant change is easily exaggerated, however, as women's wages were not high and certainly not equal to those of men.[28]

Still, a considerable number of women were going out into the world and making it on their own, and this gave them the opportunity to expand their freedom. They were able to compete in organized sports, to wear comfortable clothes, and to expect sexual fulfillment. At times during the 1920s women engaged in activities that shocked their elders and, especially,

---

[27] Allen, *A Century to Celebrate*, 337; Banner, *Women in Modern America*, 45, 47–48.

[28] William Henry Chafe, *The American Woman: Her Changing Social, Economic, and Political Roles, 1920–1970* (New York: Oxford University Press, 1972) 50–51, 65.

their ministers. By and large Southern Baptists opposed the Nineteenth Amendment and what followed in its wake. The thoroughly sexist editor of the *Western Recorder*, J. W. Porter, said, "The feminine demons, knowingly or otherwise, are pointing womankind to the path that leads to harlotry and to hell." Although Porter probably represented the thinking of many Southern Baptist men, it must be pointed out that some Southern Baptists, like editor James B. Gambrell of the *Baptist Standard* (the journal of Texas Baptists) and J. M. Dawson, pastor of the First Baptist Church in Temple, Texas, favored woman's suffrage. Gambrell saw it as inevitable and opposing it as futile, while Dawson was convinced that giving women the right to vote would have a positive influence on the social and political life of the country.[29]

When women going to the polls was followed by women assuming shocking social liberties in the 1920s, various religious leaders, particularly fundamentalists of all denominations, were horror-stricken and uttered dire predictions that the country would soon be in a moral freefall. In 1919 a male Alabamian had argued that woman's suffrage would lead to moral corruption, confusion, degeneracy, and the final downfall of the nation. Members of the Alabama Legislature listened and believed, and, for the second time, they voted against ratifying the Nineteenth Amendment. Between 1920 and 1925 fundamentalists hurled sharp barbs at liberated young women called flappers, assailing them for "immodest dress, improper dancing, frequenting immoral plays, and indulging in smoking, gambling, swearing, and joyriding."[30]

---

[29] Banner, *Women in Modern America*, 171; Bill Sumners, "Southern Baptist Women and Women's Right to Vote, 1910–1920," *Baptist History & Heritage* (January 1977): 48–50.

[30] DeBerg, *Ungodly Women*, 107; Flynt and Berkley, *Taking Christianity to China*, 28.

Not all fundamentalists, however, were antifeminists. A few fundamentalists supported the vote for women, but for every one who did, approximately ten others were opposed. Most took the position held by a fundamentalist evangelist named T. DeWitt Talmage that women could do more for God by staying out of the workplace and out of public affairs. A notable exception among Northern Baptists was the prominent John Roach Straton. He waved the fundamentalist banner as enthusiastically as anyone, and yet he favored woman's suffrage and welcomed a woman evangelist and Bible teacher named Uldine Uttley to preach in his pulpit. Conservative Southern Baptists were outraged by Straton's stance, calling it a "flagrant violation of the clear teaching of the Scripture."[31]

As Southern Baptists continued to stand firm on a literal rendering of the Bible, other denominations were showing signs of a broader perspective. There was increasing agitation to integrate women missionary societies into the general foreign mission boards, since women seemed to be in competition with those boards. In 1910 the Methodist Episcopal Church South merged its two general and two women's boards into a single Board of Missions. This board had within it a "Women's Council," and women were given membership and secretarial posts supposedly in equal proportion to men. Around the same time, the Congregationalists and the Presbyterians consolidated their mission work. Northern Baptists would not merge with the women's mission society in their denomination until 1954, and Southern Baptists never merged with the WMU because neither sought nor wanted such a union. Although Northern Baptists were slow to merge their mission efforts with the women's mission society in their ranks, they did elect a woman as president of their convention. She was Helen Barrett

---

[31] DeBerg, *Ungodly Women*, 51, 56–57; Janette Hassey, *No Time for Silence: Evangelical Women in Public Ministry around the Turn of the Century* (Grand Rapids MI: Academie Books, 1986) 118.

Montgomery, and she was president in 1921 when a dispute between fundamentalists and regulars over theology almost split the Northern Baptist Convention. Ironically, Montgomery fought unsuccessfully against the mergers of women's missionary societies with denominational mission boards, for she feared that such mergers would erode the power base that women's missions efforts had attained within American churches. The women's societies of four major Protestant denominations lost their institutional autonomy, as Montgomery had predicted. The WMU of Southern Baptist women, however, remained "auxiliary" to the Southern Baptist Convention and thus held on to its autonomy.[32]

As the gender struggle continued in various denominations, American women won a great secular political victory near the end of the second decade of the twentieth century with the ratification of the Nineteenth Amendment. For the first time, in 1920, women throughout America voted in the election to choose the president of the United States. This was the election that prompted one newspaper editor to admonish Americans to go to the polls, hold their noses, vote, and then go home and get down on their knees and thank God that only one of the candidates could be elected. It has been alleged that women voted overwhelmingly for the Republican candidate, handsome Warren G. Harding, whom, according to some historians, was one of our most intellectually-challenged presidents. He clearly had trouble getting a handle on the job, as his administration became one of the most scandal-ridden in all of American history. Some people have taken the election of Harding and the his scandals to mean that women were to blame, since they were inferior to men in understanding politics and simply voted for the man because he was handsome. Such a contention is clearly ridiculous, for men as

---

[32] Beaver, *American Protestant Women in World Mission*, 180, 184–87; Hill, *The World Their Household*, 6, 161, 167, 183.

well as women voted for Harding, and men as well as women voted for the loser, Democratic candidate James M. Cox.

The combined votes of men and women put Harding in the White House, and men as well as women were responsible for the so-called "Roaring Twenties" that followed during the Harding years and those of his successor, Calvin Coolidge. Just because women raised the lengths of their skirts, shortened the length of their hair, began to use cosmetics, dared to smoke cigarettes and drink alcoholic beverages, and had their fun dancing the Charleston, the world was not about to end, even though many conservatives of various religious persuasions were certain that it was. Not a few men were sure that the women's movement had put the nation on the pathway to ruin, but the women who made good use of their new-found freedom usually enjoyed it *with men* who had liberal attitudes. Besides, the loudest roars of the twenties were heard in urban America. The rest of the country experienced little change.

Unquestionably the old attitudes of the Victorian age were being battered, and women were making some progress toward equality. At the same time, however, women disagreed among themselves, sometimes vehemently, over how far they should go in seeking equality. The quarrel was precipitated by the proposal of an Equal Rights Amendment to the United States Constitution in 1923, and the emotional antagonism provoked by it lasted through the twenties and into the thirties. The debate was in full swing when the blight of the Great Depression settled on America from coast to coast and from the Great Lakes to the Gulf of Mexico, and people struggled simply to survive. The pace of the movement for women's rights was thus significantly slowed during the 1930s.

In spite of the hard times that characterized the 1930s, the attitude prevailed in many quarters that married women, at least, ought not to work. Economic necessity undercut that attitude, and more women found employment. Then, in the early 1940s, with the onset of World War II, the number of women in the workplace increased dramatically. They took the jobs of men who had gone off to war. Rosie the Riveter became the highly acclaimed symbol of women at work. Many people, however, assumed this was a temporary development. It was somewhat disconcerting to conservatives when some women began to agitate for equal pay and especially when the federal government paid lip service to that idea.[33]

When the men returned from war, it was expected that the women would go back home and resume their traditional roles as wife and mother. Reaction soon set in against the idea of the liberated woman. Marriage and motherhood were heralded as the proper role for women. Antifeminist rhetoric was often heard. Women were openly blamed for society's ills because they had left the home to work and had failed as mothers. A back-to-the-home movement got underway, as America sought to return to its patriarchal past.[34]

In 1947 a reactionary work titled *Modern Woman: The Lost Sex* was published. Its authors were Ferdinand Lundberg and Marynia Farnham. They argued that the influence of the "masculine woman" should be curbed and that women should accept their "higher role" as modern wives and mothers. Other writers, even some females, began echoing similar sentiments.[35]

Meanwhile, throughout the 1920s, 1930s, and 1940s fundamentalists of different denominations, and certainly Southern Baptist fundamentalists, had never stopped asserting that women were inferior to men and ought to submit to their control. W. P. Harvey, a contributor to J. W. Porter's book called *Feminism: Woman and Her Work*, wrote, "What is called the 'Woman's Movement' is the most insidious and malicious

---

[33] Banner, *Women in Modern America*, 191, 196, 202–204.

[34] Ibid., 211–12, 216–17; Chafe, *The American Woman*, 139–42, 151–73 passim, 178.

[35] Chafe, *The American Woman*, 203–207.

conspiracy ever concocted against the inspiration of the Bible and our Christian homes." Another contributor to Porter's antifeminist anthology was W. H. Felix, who wrote, "She is not to speak in public and assume political rights to vote and hold office, because the Scriptures say it leads to the ignoring of her subjection and obedience. It is the assumption of authority over the man.... I appeal to the women of our churches to adhere unfalteringly to the old way." Porter himself wrote, "The woman's Rights, Anti-slavery, and Social Equality movements were rocked in the same cradle, and fostered by the same friends." He accused feminists of trying to be men, being immodest, conspiring to lower the birth rate (and succeeding at it), causing the divorce rate to climb, promoting licentiousness, and committing crimes. Another fundamentalist Baptist, John R. Rice, wrote a book called *Bobbed Hair, Bossy Wives, and Women Preachers* in which he contended that a woman's glory lay in being "a help to a man, and in submission to her husband or her father." Rice, one of the most blatant male chauvinists ever to mount a pulpit, wrote a whole book to say one thing, and that was that women should be subordinate to men at all times: case closed.[36]

With attitudes such as these appearing regularly for over three decades in the printed word published by a variety of religious leaders, plus the fact that most mainline Protestant denominations were holding the line against women being ordained or being given leadership roles in the churches, it is understandable that gaining the vote and a measure of social freedom were the last major advances women made until the 1960s and 1970s. A bit ahead of some other denominations, the Presbyterian Church USA did ordain a woman to the ministry in

---

[36] J. W. Porter, ed., *Feminism: Woman and Her Work* (Louisville: Baptist Book Concern, 1923) 10, 24–40 passim, 73, 118; John R. Rice, *Bobbed Hair, Bossy Wives, and Women Preachers* (Wheaton IL: Sword of the Lord Publishers, 1941) 15–16, 52, 68.

1956. The Episcopal Church eventually followed suit, and by the mid-1980s had more than 400 priests, but on the whole that denomination, like the others, moved slowly on women's issues. During the 1960s and 1970s American women of all religious persuasions—Protestants, Jews, and Catholics, too—were finally spurred into action by the resurgence of the women's movement, and they sought "to find their religious and female roots."[37]

The 1960s and1970s became intense decades when the Women's Liberation movement caused women to protest loudly against their continuing subordination in the churches. They in effect insisted on equal opportunity in theological education and ordination. Most denominations recognized that male domination was headed for the scrap heap of history and yielded. Two Lutheran denominations began ordaining women in 1970. The Episcopal Church submitted to the inevitable in 1976, but the issue created a schism. No progress was made in the Roman Catholic Church, and very little was realized among Protestant fundamentalists, who continued their adamant opposition to women being ordained. A few Southern Baptist churches defied their sister churches and took the big step of ordaining women to the pastoral ministry, but as a whole the denomination remained firmly opposed to women pastors.[38]

The gains toward equality that women did make were due more to the federal government and labor unions than to the churches. Women's contributions to the nation during World War II had prompted the government to endorse their right to equal pay. At the same time, labor unions committed themselves to helping women workers in their struggle for fair treatment in the workplace. Finally, in 1973, Congress passed the Equal Rights Amendment, fifty years after it had first been introduced, and sent it to the states for ratification as an amendment to the

---

[37] Greaves, *Triumph over Silence*, 11–12, 252–55; Lindley, *"You have Stept Out of Your Place,"* ix.

[38] Beaver, *American Protestant Women in World Mission*, 212.

United States Constitution. Ratification required the vote of thirty-eight state legislatures, but only thirty-six states approved it, and the amendment went down to defeat. Interestingly enough, conservative women like Phyllis Schlafly, a rightwing activist, were to some extent responsible for this result.[39]

Reactionaries poured from the cracks of American society like termites during the struggle over the Equal Rights Amendment and, especially, following the US Supreme Court's *Roe v. Wade* decision, handed down the same year that Congress passed the ERA. That highly controversial decision legalized abortion in the United States, and abortion was anathema to many religious groups. Fundamentalist Baptist preacher Jerry Falwell of Lynchburg, Virginia, was spurred into action. He founded an organization called the Moral Majority, which was dedicated to overturning *Roe v. Wade* and securing the election to office of rightwing politicians who would support its cause. Falwell and his followers sought to counter what they regarded as evil influences in American culture, influences that threatened "to subvert the fundamentalists' ideal of femininity." The fundamentalists were certain that the legalization of abortion clearly demonstrated that American culture had abandoned that ideal, although nothing in the Bible specifically dictates a pro-life stance.[40]

How far did women progress in the twentieth century toward equality with men? That remains a debatable question, but it is quite clear that the struggle goes on. Conservatives contend that women have made considerable progress, particularly in the workplace and in education, while militant feminists emphasize what has not been gained.[41] While the debate and struggle go on, a number of conclusions appear to be obvious. The churches,

---

[39] Banner, *Women in Modern America*, 171, 247–48.
[40] John S. Hawley, ed., *Fundamentalism and Gender* (New York: Oxford University Press, 1994) 56, 58.
[41] Banner, *Women in Modern America*, 236–42.

with a small number of notable exceptions, have done little to help women in their struggle for equality either in society at large or within their own organizations. Societal attitudes that assigned to women the role of submissive wives, dedicated mothers, and quiet homemakers were staunchly reinforced by all the major denominations for decades and by the Southern Baptist Convention throughout the century. Even though most of the major Protestant denominations finally saw the light and recognized that women's claims to equality were just, Southern Baptists, like Catholics and Mormons, insisted on strongly affirming the traditional attitudes. In fact, Southern Baptists formalized their reactionary stance during the last two decades of the century by passing resolutions at their annual conventions, resolutions that denied women leadership roles in the denomination. In particular, women were to be submissive to their husbands and were forbidden to seek ordination as deacons or ministers. Thus, the Southern Baptist Convention ended the twentieth century as it had begun it, clearly committed to a *modus operandi* of male domination.

CHAPTER 2

"A MIASMA OF SCANDAL"

RADICAL WOMEN ACTIVISTS AND SOUTHERN BAPTISTS

Southern Baptists, women as well as men, have always been conservative people. Mavericks among them, men and women, have appeared from time to time, but they have been relatively few. Most Southern Baptists of both sexes tend to regard unconventional people and abrasive radicals with suspicion. For this reason, radical women activists had about as much to do with the unassertiveness of Southern Baptist women as did the attitude of Southern Baptist men. Not that many Southern Baptist women—perhaps none—were calling for woman's suffrage in the years immediately following the Civil War, but if some were thinking about it, they were almost certainly turned away from the idea by the type of people in the North who advocated it. The leading advocates were Susan B. Anthony, Elizabeth Cady Stanton, Lucretia Mott, and Victoria Woodhull. A leading male advocate was Henry Ward Beecher, pastor of the Plymouth Church (Congregational) in Brooklyn. Beecher was one of the most highly acclaimed preachers in the United States. When he was accused of adultery with one of his church members in 1871, the news of the affair spread quickly in woman-suffrage circles, and "a miasma of scandal engulfed the cause." Although Beecher's alleged affair caused him to resign as president of the American Woman Suffrage Association, the damage was done in the eyes of many, especially those who had not looked favorably upon the cause in the first place. Besides the Beecher affair, there were rumors that many women in the women's rights movement had affairs with prominent men. Moreover, some of the most publicized women in the movement owned friendship with Victoria Woodhull, a notorious advocate of free love.[1]

Since dinner conversations are seldom recorded for posterity, one can only guess how many times a Southern Baptist husband, during the closing years of the nineteenth century, told his wife over the evening meal that she was fortunate not to live among such reprobates as those women's rights crusaders. More than a few warnings must have been issued to Southern women, Baptists and others, to the effect that venturing into too much public activity by women could only turn them into the likes of Susan Anthony, Elizabeth Stanton, and, God forbid, Victoria Woodhull! One is reminded of the Reverend Mr. Oliver Blue of Alabama who called feminist Lucy Stone "very little above a common strumpet." No doubt many Southern men expressed similar sentiments on more than one occasion, and it has been noted that Southern women took pride in being ladylike and doing what their husbands expected of them. Their men surely expected them to behave differently from northern feminists.

The origins and development of feminism in America were used as tools by Southern Baptist men to help persuade women to accept their prescribed role and their subordinate status. Some of

---

[1] Barbara Goldsmith, *Other Powers: The Age of Suffrage, Spiritualism, and the Scandalous Victoria Woodhull* (New York: Alfred A. Knopf, 1998) 281–82.

the women in early America who stepped out and courageously urged their sisters to stand up for their rights have only recently begun to be recognized as heroines. For most of American history they have been regarded simply as uppity women who did not know or refused to accept their rightful place. The first such woman in America was Anne Hutchinson, who troubled the peace of Boston during its founding years. Born in England in 1591, this remarkable woman, who insisted on her right to interpret and teach the Bible, married William Hutchinson in 1612 and bore him fifteen children. Mrs. Hutchinson was a devout Puritan, and she came to believe that there were only two "true preachers" in England. They were her own minister, John Cotton, and her brother-in-law, John Wheelwright. When Cotton was forced out of England in 1633, the Hutchinsons followed him to New England in 1634. There the presumptuous Mrs. Hutchinson stirred up a controversy that had its roots in both theology and political power.[2] Hutchinson's assertiveness led to her banishment from the Massachusetts colony. She and her followers founded a colony in what later became Rhode Island, but she did not leave her contentiousness behind in Boston, and her colony became too small for her and some of her followers to dwell together in peace. Eventually, she moved on to New York where she and some of her children were killed by Indians. Regarded as a troublemaker in her own time, Hutchinson has come to be looked upon in recent years as a heroine for being the first woman in America to speak up for women's rights.

There were other religious women who also made a public statement. Quaker women, for example, did not hesitate to go where they were not wanted and spread the teachings of George Fox. Mary Dyer, a Quaker who had once been a follower of Anne

---

[2] Janet W. James, ed., *Women in American Religion* (Philadelphia: University of Pennsylvania Press, 1976) 3; Susan Hill Lindley, *"You Have Stept Out of Your Place:" A History of Women and Religion in America* (Louisville: Westminster/John Knox Press, 1996) 2–3.

Hutchinson, was hanged in Boston in 1660, when she returned after being run out of town several times. A little over a century later, Mother Ann Lee founded the Shaker sect with its communal living and peculiar doctrine of sexual abstinence. In spite of being persecuted, Mother Ann traveled and proclaimed her views. She won converts who established churches in several parts of America. Ann Lee died in 1784.[3]

What effect did such women as Hutchinson, Dyer, and Lee have on America's religious women? Though it cannot be documented, those women were probably a source of encouragement to other women who felt they should have a voice in church affairs. If Susan Juster is right in saying that Baptist women in New England did participate in making church decisions during most of the eighteenth century, the examples set by the radical women mentioned above must have provided their Baptist sisters and other women in evangelical churches some inspiration. Women in the established churches—Congregational in New England and Anglican in the Southern colonies—were more restricted and enjoyed no more than an informal influence in their churches. The point is that there were enough radical women in colonial America, and their deeds made a deep enough impression, to set a precedent for the women who launched the crusade for women's rights in the nineteenth century. Put another way, Anne Hutchinson, Mary Dyer, and Ann Lee were precursors of Lucy Stone, Lucretia Mott, Elizabeth Cady Stanton, Susan B. Anthony, and Victoria Woodhull. In the meantime, the conservative Anglican South had been replaced by the conservative Baptist and Methodist South, and both Baptists—especially Southern Baptists—and Methodists found radicalism, particularly female radicalism, as repulsive as

---

[3] Harry N. Hollis, Jr. and others, *Christian Freedom for Women and Other Human Beings* (Nashville: Broadman Press, 1974) 21–24; Amanda Porterfield, *Feminine Spirituality in America* (Philadelphia: Temple University Press, 1980) 37–39, 69–75, 119–22, 125–28, 155–58.

eighteenth-century conservatives of the New England and Southern colonies had found them.

To say that there was no assertion of women's rights before the Seneca Falls Convention in 1848 would be a mistake, but it is true that the women's movement was given a clearly delineated form and some semblance of organization by that momentous gathering. Some reformers earlier in the century had denied that women were inferior to men and had urged young women to consider themselves as equal to any man. Lucy Stone, one of the trailblazers for women's rights, refused to have the word "obey" in her marriage vows or to give up her name for her husband's.

While the women who spawned the women's rights movement were not, socioeconomically speaking, from the dregs of American society, they were far removed from the mainstream of American life. Many of them had participated in the abolition and temperance movements, and they were often treated as outcasts. The radical nature of their movement was revealed in the Declaration of Sentiments and Resolutions passed at Seneca Falls. That document declared that all men *and* women were created equal, and it indicted mankind for its "history of repeated injuries and usurpations" toward women by not allowing them political representation or permitting them to own property. Women, it declared, were oppressed by men "on all sides." A resolution was unanimously passed calling for the "overthrow of the monopoly of the pulpit." Both Quaker Lucretia Mott and Methodist Anna Howard Shaw preached at the convention, thus further dramatizing the women's demand for equal religious rights. The demand, however, that would create the biggest controversy over the next seven decades was the demand for giving women the right to vote. The suffrage came to symbolize feminism more than any other issue, for it indicated that women were ready to break out of the narrow sphere to which their lives had been assigned and to establish themselves as independent beings. Women wanted the vote for another reason—it would enable them to help bring about, through legislation, reforms that they believed were needed.[4] Such radical ideas, coming from people who supported abolitionism, were not likely to be viewed favorably in the South by women and certainly not by men, who had created an economic way of life dependent upon slavery. Seneca Falls came three years after the founding of the Southern Baptist Convention, and the radicals who sponsored the gathering in New York essentially declared war on many things that were dear to Southern Baptist hearts, including the right to own slaves.

During the Civil War the nation's attention was diverted from women's issues, but immediately after the war ended, the suffragist movement reignited its cause. Soon thereafter the movement became embroiled in a series of events that led to quarrels, splits, and scandals. At the American Equal Rights Convention in 1869 differing views led to an acrimonious split into the National Woman Suffrage Association, led by Elizabeth Cady Stanton, and the American Woman Suffrage Association, led by Lucy Stone. Henry Ward Beecher, among other famous men, supported Stone's organization and became its president. Theodore Tilton, who was editor of the *Brooklyn Daily Union* and a member of Beecher's church, was president of the rival organization.[5]

---

[4] William Henry Chafe, *The American Woman: Her Changing Social, Economic, and Political Roles, 1920–1970* (New York: Oxford University Press, 1972) 3–5; Jill K.Conway, *The Female Experience in Eighteenth and Nineteenth Century America: A Guide to the History of American Women* (New York and London: Garland Publishing Co., 1982) 199; Nancy F. Cott, *The Bonds of Womanhood* (New Haven: Yale University Press, 1977) 153–55; Richard L. Greaves, ed., *Triumph over Silence: Women in Protestant History* (Westport CT and London: Greenwood Press, 1985) 10–11; Anne Firor Scott, *The Southern Lady: From Pedestal to Politics, 1830–1930* (Chicago and London: University of Chicago Press, 1970) 165, 170.

[5] Goldsmith, *Other Powers*, 214–18, 223–26, 228–29.

The split in the suffrage movement was damaging enough without the dramatic scandal that soon became associated with it. In 1868 Beecher allegedly began a love affair with Theodore Tilton's wife, Elizabeth Richards (Lib) Tilton. Tilton himself had a mistress, Laura Curtis Bullard, who decided in 1870 that changing divorce and marriage laws was more important to women's freedom than was the suffrage. That same year Lib Tilton became pregnant. Apparently Tilton thought at first that he had impregnated his wife and talked Lib into an open marriage, which led briefly to his wife and his mistress becoming close friends. Tilton reconsidered his open marriage proposal when he learned that Beecher was the father of Lib's unborn child. News of all of this began to circulate in 1871, and over the next five years the entire nation would learn that two of the most prominent male supporters of the woman's suffrage movement were adulterers. To make matters worse, Victoria Woodhull, the brazenly open advocate of free love and licensed prostitution, would hook up with the suffrage movement. Even some of the most progressive suffragists were aghast at having Woodhull associated with their cause. Feminists quickly lost much support, and the protracted Beecher-Tilton scandal continued to cause more damage.[6]

Not only did Tilton have a mistress, he became involved with Victoria Woodhull. He wrote a biography of her, and during the summer of 1871, he practiced free love with her, spending many nights at her house and sleeping with her "on the cool rooftop." Woodhull claimed that Henry Ward Beecher, too, though not an avowed advocate of free love, was a practical free lover "who kept a harem in Brooklyn and had more illegitimate children than any other man in town." The controversial Woodhull was determined to tar Beecher with the free-love brush and make sure that the world knew he was an adulterer. On 2

---

[6] Chafe, *The American Woman*, 11; Goldsmith, *Other Powers*, 263, 281.

November 1872, she published "The Beecher-Tilton Scandal Case" and circulated it in 100,000 copies of *Woodhull & Claflin's Weekly*. This story contained the salacious details of Beecher's affair with Mrs. Tilton.[7]

Meanwhile, on 20 November 1871, Victoria Woodhull delivered a speech at Steinway Hall in New York City. Her address, titled "The Principles of Social Freedom," led to questions from the audience. When asked if she were a free lover, she responded that she was. Pandemonium broke out in the auditorium. The audience hissed at her and loudly denounced her. The next day one newspaper declared, "Died of Free Love...The Woman Suffrage Movement."[8]

Apparently Woodhull and her cohort in free love, Theodore Tilton, were more committed to ruining Henry Ward Beecher than to minimizing harm to the suffrage movement. Both of them continued to charge Beecher with adultery, and on 10 July 1874, Tilton appeared before a committee of Plymouth Church to lodge a formal accusation against the famous pulpiteer. Tilton gave an account of Beecher's adulterous relationship with Lib Tilton, offering many letters and documents to support his case. When Tilton took this step, Lib left him and tried to clear Beecher, who soon denied everything. The heralded preacher then charged Tilton with having become corrupted through his association with Victoria Woodhull. There is strong evidence that Beecher was guilty of the charges, but he had not been so foolish—as Tilton had—to avow free love. Whatever he and Lib Tilton had done, they did not declare it publicly. Furthermore, since Beecher picked the committee that heard Tilton's charges, the outcome was predictable. On 22 August 1874, after all the stories had been told and all the evidence had been presented, the church committee announced that they found their minister

---

[7] Goldsmith, *Other Powers*, 289–90, 293, 337.
[8] Ibid., 303–304.

innocent and declared that Henry Ward Beecher had been exonerated.[9]

The Plymouth Church committee publicly read its report to an audience of 3,400 with hundreds more standing outside the church. Beecher was pronounced guiltless, while Tilton was branded as a practitioner of "infidelity" who had "free love proclivities." Only one man opposed the report, and he was threatened with death by the crowd.[10]

After Beecher's church found him innocent of adultery, Theodore Tilton filed suit against the minister in civil court, charging him with alienation of affection and demanding $100,000 in damages. The trial began on 11 January 1875 and went on until 2 July of the same year. It was front-page news for 112 days. The final outcome was a mistrial with jurors voting 9 to 3 against Tilton.[11]

The Beecher-Tilton scandal did not single-handedly disrupt the women's rights movement in the 1870s and 1880s, but it contributed significantly to the squabbling that caused the movement to remain divided and to make little or no progress for close to two decades. It caused conservatives throughout the country to look askance at any activity undertaken by women. In order to get anywhere in promoting their cause of supporting mission work, women in the more conservative denominations, especially in the South, had to assure a fearful male leadership that the organizations they wanted to establish were not the first step toward radical feminism or women's rights. Southern Baptists strenuously opposed the women's movement in general and the suffrage movement in particular, believing that the vote for women would lead to female degradation and the destruction of the home and nation. Women might next want to hold public

---

[9] Ibid., 389–95, 403.
[10] Ibid., 405–10.
[11] Ibid., 410, 411, 416.

office and thus be dragged into the corrupt game of politics.[12] After all the adverse publicity that the suffrage movement received as a result of the Beecher-Tilton scandal and the movement's association with Victoria Woodhull and free love, it is virtually certain that women were discouraged from too much public activity by conservative husbands all over America.

Not until 1890 did the woman's suffrage movement begin to right itself and move forward again. After eighteen years of feuding, the women's groups were reunited as the National American Woman Suffrage Association. The women dropped some of their more explosive issues, such as women's right to divorce and their right to be free from exploitation in the workplace. The movement was to concentrate mainly on the suffrage. Almost alone, Elizabeth Cady Stanton held out for more than this, arguing that the right to vote was only "the vestibule of woman's emancipation." She died in 1902 at the age of eighty-six, but during the 1890s she came out with her *Woman's Bible*, a work that was to diminish her influence with most religious women who claimed to be Christians. She attacked established religion for making women subject to men. Few women at that time were willing to attack the Bible and Christianity in the radical way she did. To her the New Testament was no better than the Old since both had been used to keep women in a separate and subordinate sphere. She wrote: "The Bible teaches that woman brought sin and death into the world, that she precipitated the fall of the race, that she was arraigned before the judgment seat of Heaven, tried, condemned and sentenced...in silence and subjection, she was to play the role of a dependent on man's bounty for all her material wants."[13]

---

[12] Lindley, *You Have Stept Out of Your Place*, 86; Scott, *The Southern Lady*, 137; Rufus Spain, *At Ease in Zion: A Social History of Southern Baptists, 1865–1900* (Nashville: Vanderbilt University Press, 1961) 167.

[13] Chafe, *The American Woman*, 7, 15; Goldsmith, *Other Powers*, 434–35; Lindley, *You Have Stept Out of Your Place*, 275, 290.

With one of the *granddames* of the women's rights movement making such declarations against the Bible, one does not have to wonder why Southern Baptist women were not supporters—at least the vast majority of them—of woman's suffrage.

In spite of all that Stanton and other radical women did to inflame conservatives everywhere, women did become more active during the 1890s. Frances Willard and her organization, the Women's Christian Temperance Union, launched an attack against saloons and alcoholism. The WCTU came to have over two million members, and before long the membership went beyond its temperance crusade to call for child labor reform, prison reform, the establishment of homes for unwed mothers, woman's suffrage, and—in some cases—socialism. Simultaneously, women's clubs began to multiply and to advocate various reforms—even in the South. By 1914 most of the women's organizations were focused on achieving the right to vote. Conservative Protestant churches and especially the Catholic Church opposed the women's demands for the vote. The fears of conservative men were realized when a few women actually moved into politics after 1910. Some women in the Democratic party gained local and state offices. As disturbing as this was, it seemed less serious to some men than did the work of Margaret Sanger, a radical feminist, who began to demand that women be allowed to choose and practice birth control.[14]

Conservatives no doubt thought that the world was truly turning upside down in 1919 when the Nineteenth Amendment

---

[14] Lois W. Banner, *Women in Modern America: A Brief History* (New York: Harcourt, Brace, and Jovanovich, 1974) 87–88, 94, 102–103; Betty A. DeBerg, *Ungodly Women: Gender and the First Wave of American Fundamentalism* (Minneapolis: Fortress Press, 1990) 28–30; Wayne Flynt and Gerald Berkley, *Taking Christianity to China: Alabama Missionaries in the Middle Kingdom, 1850–1950* (Tuscaloosa and London: University of Alabama Press, 1997) 201; Joane V. Hawks and Sheila L. Skemp, eds., *Sex, Race, and the Role of Women in the South* (Jackson: University of Mississippi Press, 1983) 107–109; Scott, *The Southern Lady*, 150–51, 162.

passed the US House of Representatives by a vote of 304 to 90 and the Senate by 56 to 25. The following year that momentous addition to the US Constitution was ratified by the states. This great victory allowed women all over America to cast their ballots, but it brought mixed results. Although women used their right to vote to assert themselves and push for leadership roles, various women's groups splintered and lost their central focus. The National American Woman's Suffrage Association disbanded. Still, at least one woman had served in every state legislature except that of Louisiana by 1930, and in 1935 "Ma" Ferguson became the first woman governor when she was chosen by the Texas electorate.[15]

For many women the right to vote was the only reform needed, Elizabeth Cady Stanton's arguments to the contrary notwithstanding. Hence, when they got the franchise, the preponderance of American women were satisfied. Thus, when the Equal Rights Amendment was proposed in 1923 as a means of providing women with full equality, squabbling among various women's groups over objectives erupted. It was the 1870s and 1880s all over again, only this time the acrimony was not precipitated by personal scandal involving key people in the women's rights movement. To some extent the previous disputes were rooted in philosophical differences, but not to the degree caused by the introduction of the ERA. Strong disagreement over the merits of the proposed amendment would continue for five decades. Once again, extreme behavior turned society away from granting greater freedom to women. The roaring twenties saw young people revolt against Victorian morality. They engaged in shocking behavior, causing many to ask questions such as, "Is this what freedom for women is all about?" A new antifeminism

---

[15] Banner, *Women in Modern America*, 125, 131–32, 134; Chafe, *The American Woman*, 20–22; Sheila M. Rothman, *Woman's Proper Place: A History of Changing Ideals and Practices, 1870 to the Present* (New York: Basic Books, 1978) 38.

arose, as most people concluded that freedom for women had gone quite far enough. Even though more women did venture into the workplace, there were setbacks. American labor, as well as American women, lost favor with the public, and union membership declined. Even so, the ERA continued to have supporters, and when Franklin D. Roosevelt won the presidency and initiated the New Deal in 1933, the ERA found a champion: Eleanor Roosevelt, the nation's first lady. Mrs. Roosevelt was no Elizabeth Cady Stanton sounding a tocsin for radical change, but the fact that she was the first lady of the land and dared speak out forthrightly for the rights of women did not set well with conservatives—men or women. Despite the conservative mood of the country, by 1944 both political parties had endorsed the ERA, yet it would be nearly thirty more years before it passed Congress.[16]

Although President Roosevelt was not as visible as his wife in promoting women's rights, he was almost surely sympathetic to her views, as was indicated by his naming the first woman to the Cabinet. She was Frances Perkins, who became secretary of labor. According to Mary Anderson, who headed the Women's Bureau, Perkins did everything she could to avoid pushing for the cause of women. Yet, her presence as a Cabinet member helped the cause of women's rights.[17]

World War II drove women into the workplace to do the jobs of men who had gone off to war, and when the war was over a "back-to-the-home movement" for women was soon underway. There was a clear call from conservatives in American society for women to return to their traditional role of wife, mother, and homemaker. Southern Baptist men had taken this position before the passage of the Nineteenth Amendment. They had strongly opposed woman's suffrage, and upon despairing of preventing it,

---

[16] Banner, *Women in Modern America*, 141–42, 146, 155–60, 173–74; Chafe, *The American Woman*, 46–47, 112–113.

[17] Banner, *Women in Modern America*, 179–80.

they had urged the women of the South to resist the appeals of the "bold and unprincipled women" from the North who were responsible for all the social agitation. At the height of the suffrage agitation, when Congress was on the brink of passing the Nineteenth Amendment, J. W. Porter had linked the pro-woman faction in the SBC to Susan B. Anthony and especially to the kind of biblical interpretation found in Elizabeth Cady Stanton's *Woman's Bible.* Southern Baptist men had been sure from the outset that all desire of Southern Baptist women to organize and participate was spawned by outside agitators from the North—those radicals who favored woman's suffrage and other rights for women. Plainly put, the South, in large part because of Southern Baptists, had to be dragged into the light of the twentieth century.[18] Even when women won the vote, Southern Baptist men wanted that to be the end of reform, and for all practical purposes, it was for almost forty years.

Even though the movement for women's rights resembled a mouse's squeak more than a lion's roar after the ratification of the Nineteenth Amendment and the passing into history of the roaring twenties, the worst was yet to come for conservatives who wanted women to remain quietly on the sidelines of American society. The "back-to-the-home" movement of the late 1940s and early 1950s ran into a roadblock in the early 1960s, when women became militant in demanding equal rights with men. In 1963 Betty Friedan published *The Feminine Mystique,* which was a call to battle for women activists. Friedan demanded the liberation of women from the boring role of housewife and mother. Romanticizing domesticity was a sham, as far as Friedan was concerned. In her eyes the domestic role

---

[18] Catherine B. Allen, *A Century to Celebrate: History of Woman's Missionary Union* (Birmingham AL: Woman's Missionary Union, 1987) 31; DeBerg, *Ungodly Women*, 84–85; Scott, *The Southern Lady*, 184, 187–89, 197, 199–201, 211; Spain, *At Ease in Zion*, 165–68; *Western Recorder*, 27 March 1919, 8.

amounted to "voluntary servitude." Few would doubt that *The Feminine Mystique* contained more than several exaggerations, but it struck a responsive chord with American women. Women could see clearly now that they did not possess equal rights, and they were made aware that, at this juncture, the ERA had been endorsed by both major political parties and promoted by neither. If women were going to have equal rights, they had to demand them and work to get them.[19]

Action followed words, and the Women's Liberation movement, or "Women's Lib," was launched. Friedan led in founding the National Organization of Women (NOW) in 1966. Actually NOW was made up of professional women and was one of the more moderate of the Women's Lib groups. Some of the groups made up of younger, more radical women called for revolutionary change, while NOW took a reformist approach. Women's Lib made common cause with the Civil Rights movement, feeding off of its demands to eliminate prejudice and discrimination in American society. *The Feminine Mystique* was soon joined in the literary marketplace by other feminist books that fanned the fires ignited by militant feminism. Shulamith Firestone's *The Dialectics of Sex,* Robin Morgan's *Sisterhood of the Powerful,* and Germaine Greer's *The Female Eunuch* all gave the women's cause added impetus.[20]

Just as the suffragist movement, which few Southern Baptist women had enthusiastically endorsed, helped Southern Baptist women gain the right to serve and vote as messengers at the Southern Baptist Convention's annual meetings, Women's Lib helped at least some Southern Baptist women, as well as women in other denominations, by encouraging all women to rise up and demand their rights. During the 1960s women of the American

---

[19] Banner, *Women in Modern America,* 229–31; Chafe, *The American Woman,* 226–28; Hollis, *Christian Freedom for Women,* 72.

[20] Banner, *Women in Modern America,* 234–35; Chafe, *The American Woman,* 232, 233, 237–38.

Baptist Convention demanded that a woman be placed in the hierarchy of the denomination. Even Catholic women began to insist upon change, but they realized far fewer gains than Baptist and Methodist women. The Reverend Madeline Southard, a Methodist minister in Kansas, formed the American Association of Women Ministers, which in 1970 changed its name to the International Association of Women Ministers. A few Southern Baptist women were ordained to the ministry, while a goodly number were ordained as deacons. They began calling convocations on the role of women in the SBC in 1978 and organized Southern Baptist Women in Ministry in 1983. By this time, fundamentalists were well on their way to winning control of the SBC, and soon progress toward equality for Southern Baptist women ground to a halt.[21]

Unfortunately, many Southern Baptist women saw eye to eye with the fundamentalists on the question of women's rights. The issue was raised at the annual meeting of the SBC in Portland, Oregon, in 1973, when Mrs. Richard Sappington, wife of a Houston, Texas pastor, presented a resolution condemning the Women's Liberation movement and reaffirming the traditional roles of women in church and society. The Resolutions Committee reworded and softened Mrs. Sappington's rhetoric and offered the amended resolution to the body. After considerable discussion the messengers at the convention rejected the wording of the Resolutions Committee and adopted Mrs. Sappington's stronger wording. Progressive Southern Baptist

---

[21] Chafe, *The American Woman*, 239–40; Georgia Harkness, *Women in Church and Society* (Nashville: Abingdon Press, 1972) 130; David T. Morgan, *The New Crusades, the New Holy Land: Conflict in the Southern Baptist Convention, 1969–1991* (Tuscaloosa and London: University of Alabama Press, 1996) 155–57.

women and some men were indignant over the action, but it was indicative of the antifeminist sentiment in the SBC.[22]

During the last quarter of the twentieth century, Conservative Southern Baptist men—particularly the fundamentalists—were as adamantly opposed to and scornful of the women who launched Women's Lib in the 1960s as Southern Baptist men, during the late nineteenth and early twentieth centuries, had been opposed to and scornful of the suffragists and other women activists of their day. Southern Baptist women, generally speaking, were not thrilled with them either. A preponderance of the sisters ignored the calls of women activists for radical change in the 1960s and 1970s just as their mothers and grandmothers had ignored the suffragists decades earlier. While Southern Baptist women never joined the radical movements in any significant numbers, they still benefited from their actions. The suffragists had made American society aware that its claims to democracy were exaggerated, for the democracy excluded its women citizens from the ballot box. Consequently, progressive Southern Baptist men—of whom there were a few—saw that the same was true with regard to the SBC and managed to persuade their more conservative brothers to give women the right to serve as messengers and to vote on issues before the annual meetings. Approximately forty-five years later, when some new radical women called attention to the rights that were still denied to them as American citizens, some Southern Baptist men agreed to expand the role of women in the churches, even to the extent of ordaining women as deacons and ministers. But the fact remains, that most Southern Baptist males have consistently and deliberately thrown up barriers to women who have sought equal rights with men in the SBC. For the most part, Southern Baptist women have acquiesced for reasons that are both good and bad.

---

[22] Leon McBeth, "The Role of Women in Southern Baptist History," *Baptist History & Heritage* (January 1977): 24.

Southern Baptist women are traditionally conservative, pious and accommodating and want to be what they think the Bible and their menfolk think they should be. They have a strong desire to please, and they have been repelled by strident women who assert themselves. Knowing this about their women, Southern Baptist men have used the adherence to biblical literalism, the revulsion to radicalism, and the accommodative spirit of Southern Baptist women as means of keeping them in a subordinate position. Thus, radical women from Anne Hutchinson to Elizabeth Cady Stanton to Betty Friedan had a negative effect on Southern Baptist women by giving their husbands repulsive examples of women who stepped out of their place and who must not be emulated. Without all of those bold women, Southern Baptist women would have had a harder time gaining any ground toward equality, for those women dramatized the undemocratic features of American society and helped bring about needed reforms.

CHAPTER 3

"A SHAMEFUL ACT"

THE SOUTHERN BAPTIST CONVENTION'S
TREATMENT OF WOMEN

In 1984, when the Southern Baptist Convention held its annual
meeting in Kansas City, fundamentalists were in control. One of
the significant developments at that meeting was the passage of
Resolution Number 3, which encouraged the service of women in
all church activities "other than pastoral functions and leadership
roles entailing ordination." Bill Sherman, pastor of Woodmont
Baptist Church in Nashville, Tennessee, called Resolution
Number 3 "a shameful act." The Reverend Sadie Evans, also a
minister at Woodmont Baptist, called it "a slap in the face of
every Southern Baptist woman in the nation." Passed by a vote
of 4,793 to 3,460, it was not the first such act by the SBC, and it
was not to be the last.[1]

As indicated earlier, Southern Baptist women have always
been a part of several worlds or societies—local, Southern, and
national. The first two, as a rule, have determined their attitudes

---

[1] *The Tennessean* (1 July 1984) 2H.

and governed their actions far more than the last. While local and Southern societies usually worked in harmony with one another, both were out of step with American society more often than not. Southern society and the local societies within it were ordinarily far more conservative than that greater society, which had abolished slavery after preventing the South from preserving it. Within Southern society few institutions were more conservative than Southern Baptist churches and the Convention of which those churches were a part. Consequently, the gains that women made in American society were sometimes slow in trickling down to the women in Southern society. Oftentimes Southern Baptist women did not embrace those gains enthusiastically. Indeed, until the 1970s, the sisters in the SBC were usually unassertive because they wanted to do what was expected of them by the society in which they lived, by their male-dominated churches, and by their husbands. Moreover, their conditioning at the hands of their families, their churches, and their society caused them to spurn the radical actions of women activists.

Not all Baptist women, however, acquiesced in the role that was prescribed for them. There were always exceptions, even going back to 1639 when a Baptist woman named Catherine Scott persuaded Roger Williams to profess publicly his Baptist beliefs. Williams was later baptized, and in turn he baptized others. He went on to found the First Baptist Church in America at Providence, Rhode Island. Women at that time were not even listed on the rolls of Baptist churches in England, but in America a courageous Baptist woman—Catherine Scott—was indirectly responsible for the establishment of the first church of her faith. Very quickly women outnumbered men in American Baptist churches.[2]

---

[2] Leon McBeth, "The Role of Women in Southern Baptist History," *Baptist History & Heritage* (January 1977): 3.

In 1764, when the First Baptist Church of Philadelphia refused to allow women to participate in the election of deacons, the women held a separate meeting and framed a vigorous protest. They pointed out that they had voted since the church's founding in 1698. The men countered that women had no political voice in society and, therefore, should have none in the church. Regular Baptists throughout America soon proclaimed the subordination of women as their policy, and Regulars in the South opposed the more lenient Separate Baptists for "suffering women to pray in public."[3]

After the American Revolution, when Separate and Regular Baptist churches talked of forming a union, a major obstacle was the Regulars' objection to "the extensive ministry of women in the services" of the Separates. The obstacle was overcome in 1787, and they united as the United Baptists. The Separate tradition of allowing women to participate activly did not survive in the new union. There were no more women preachers among Baptists after 1800. Although there continued to be deaconesses, they were not allowed to speak, testify, or even vote in some churches.[4]

Thus, many years before the Southern Baptist Convention came into being, Baptist women had been, for all practical purposes, silenced and put in their place. Southern Baptists did nothing more than continue a decades-old custom of male domination in their churches. The few women who dared speak against the established order were shortly reprimanded or ostracized. Therefore, it is not surprising that no woman was listed among the approximately 300 delegates who met at the First Baptist Church of Augusta, Georgia, in May of 1845 to found the Southern Baptist Convention. The constitution of the new denomination did not specify the role of women. Indeed,

---

[3] Leon McBeth, *Women in Baptist Life* (Nashville: Broadman Press, 1979) 40–41, 45.

[4] Ibid., 45–46.

there was no mention of women. Could they serve as messengers? Could they even be members? The constitution offered no answers to these questions. A president, four vice presidents, a treasurer, and two secretaries were to be elected. Dr. William B. Johnson of South Carolina was elected president. In later years Southern Baptists would insist on calling those sent to the annual convention by the name "messengers," but in the early years the terms "delegate" and "representative" were employed regularly. Every church was entitled to send one delegate or representative per $1,000 contributed annually to the SBC, but no church was allowed more than five. It was first decided that the Convention would meet triennially, with extra meetings called if needed. That plan soon gave way to annual meetings. Since the "design" of the new Convention was "to promote Foreign and Domestic Missions, and other important objects connected with the Redeemer's kingdom," two boards were formed—the Foreign Mission Board (FMB) in Richmond, Virginia, and the Domestic Mission Board in Marion, Alabama. A third board, the Bible Board, was soon added.[5]

After ten years of development the SBC had no women serving in office or holding an appointment to any board. The Foreign Mission Board reported in 1855 on the "labors of our brethren," while mentioning no woman by her first name. Missionaries to China included George Pearcy and wife, M. T. Yates and wife, A. B. Cabaniss and wife, T. P. Crawford and wife, and G. W. Burton and wife. It was noted that "Mrs. Crawford" or "Sister Crawford" taught the Chinese how to pray. Even less was mentioned about women in the Domestic Mission Board's report. In fact, if women had any part at all in the work of this board, there was no mention of it in 1855.[6]

---

[5] *Annual of the SBC* (1845): 1, 3, 4, 11, 15, 19, 41; 1855, 3–22 passim, 24, 39.

[6] *Annual of the SBC* (1855): 24–38, 43–44, 47–58, 67–68.

Apparently the only way a woman could get her name mentioned in the official record of the SBC at that time was to give money, and even then she was identified by her husband's name or initials. At the 1855 meeting of the Convention, B. C. Pressley of South Carolina read a letter from Richard Furman, perhaps the most famous Baptist minister in South Carolina. Furman's letter had enclosed in it "a donation of one hundred dollars from Mrs. L. G. Clark[e]." On a motion offered by J. B. Jeter of Virginia, the convention thanked "sister Clarke" and divided the money among the Foreign Mission, the Domestic Mission, and the Bible Boards. Also, the treasurer's report of the Bible Board listed numerous women contributors—six from Tennessee, one from Louisiana, two from Mississippi, one from Alabama, and one from Georgia.[7]

Women, it would seem, did not actually attend the annual meeting of the SBC until 1868, when the convention was in Baltimore. Even then they were not there as messengers. Most were there to accompany their husbands, but they held a separate meeting in the home of Mrs. Ann Graves, who read to the gathering some letters from her son Rosewell Graves, a missionary to China. Rosewell's letters talked of the need for women missionaries in China, for custom there required *women* to reach Chinese women for Christ. There were already Baptist women in China, women who had accompanied their missionary husbands. Obviously there were not *enough* women from Graves's perspective, and, seemingly, he was making a plea for single women to commit as missionaries. Although one single woman had gone as a missionary to China about two decades earlier, the experiment had not worked out well. Graves must have thought that it was time to try again, but it would be four

---

[7] Ibid., 3–22 passim, 24, 39.

more years—in 1872—before single women would be endorsed for missionary work by the Committee on Woman's Work.[8]

The year 1872 was a turning point for women who wanted to become foreign missionaries. Part of the problem for years had been the board's secretary, James B. Taylor, who encouraged women to give their money to support missions. He accepted no other role for them other than going to the mission field as missionary wives—at least after the experiment with the lone single missionary woman had failed. Taylor died early in 1872 and was succeeded by Henry Allen Tupper, who made room for women in foreign missions. He persuaded the Foreign Mission Board to change its anti-woman policy. Right away Lula Whilden was allowed to accompany her married sister and her brother-in-law to China. Tupper also gained approval for Edmonia Moon, younger sister of the famous Lottie Moon, to go to China as a self-supporting missionary.[9]

Another step forward by women in 1872 occurred when Ann Graves led in forming Woman's Mission to Woman. At its annual meeting that year the SBC finally took its first recorded notice of women's work by asking the Foreign Mission Board to add to its report a section on the work of "Bible Women." The committee to which the report was referred urged "the delegates present" to organize female missionary societies in their churches. They were to select "some active, pious women" to cultivate "the missionary spirit." Two years later the FMB appointed central committees for women's work in each state. There was considerable opposition to promoting and recognizing women's work, and in some states it was strong enough to stymie the work. The opposition in North Carolina, for example, shut down the central committee for ten years. At every annual

---

[8] McBeth, "The Role of Women in Southern Baptist History," 5.

[9] Catherine B. Allen, *A Century to Celebrate: History of Woman's Missionary Union* (Birmingham AL: Woman's Missionary Union, 1987) 25–26.

meeting of the SBC from 1872 to 1888, the year in which the various women's committees emerged as a convention-wide organization called Woman's Missionary Union, there was acrimonious debate over women's work. When women's work was reported at the SBC's annual meeting, it was done by a man.[10]

In spite of the opposition to women's work in missions, the women persisted, as did Tupper. However, the FMB secretary always moved cautiously, never pushing women forward too fast. At Tupper's urging the FMB agreed to keep separate accounts of women's contributions, to foster women's societies, and to emphasize the evangelization of women, and women's work continued to grow. This was fortunate for the SBC because women actually revived Southern Baptist missionary efforts "in the gloomiest period of our suffering and privation."[11]

Persistence paid off. For whatever reason, the anti-woman sentiment that permeated the SBC subsided somewhat in the mid and late 1870s. In 1877 a woman was apparently seated as a messenger to the convention in New Orleans. She was Myra E. Graves, and she represented Brenham Baptist Church of Brenham, Texas. Her late husband, Henry Lea Graves, had served as president of Baylor University. When Mrs. Graves appeared at the convention five years later in 1882, she represented the state convention of Texas as "M. E. Graves." It is downright amazing that Mrs. Graves was seated as a messenger in 1877 and again in 1882, since the various women's missionary societies were represented at the 1877 convention by men. For example, the Woman's Missionary Society of the First Baptist Church of Richmond, Virginia, was represented by Henry A. Tupper, while the Woman's Missionary Society of the Second Baptist Church of Atlanta, Georgia, was represented by A. T. Spalding. That entire convention appears to have been the epitome of

---

[10] Ibid., 28; McBeth, "The Role of Women in Southern Baptist History," 5–6.

[11] Allen, *A Century to Celebrate*, 26–27.

ambivalence, for in the "Report on Woman's Work for Home Missions" it was asserted that: "With the rise of Christ's Kingdom on earth began the *elevation of Woman* to a full and equal share with man in all that constitutes the highest good and glory of human nature." The report went on to make a plea for using women home missionaries to convert their sisters around them who did not claim Christ as savior. The HMB "should be blessed with the special prayers and gifts and labors of our Marys and Joannas, our Dorcases, Phoebes and Priscillas. It is not to be denied that multitudes of mothers, wives, and daughters within the bounds of this Convention are almost as unenlightened in spiritual things and as degraded in habits of life as the women of China and India.[12]

If one thought that the 1877 convention was a prelude to equality for women in the Southern Baptist Convention, one would find out soon enough that women need expect to go only so far and no further. This was made quite clear at the convention in 1879 when the Committee on Woman's Work reported:

> In view of the power for good which rests with the women of *our* churches, and in view of the great needs of the work of Home and Foreign Missions, your Committee would urge the importance of enlisting as thoroughly as possible the energies of the Baptist women of the South in this great cause. While we do not approve of women's speaking before popular assemblies or in anyway usurping the duties which the New Testament imposes exclusively upon men, we yet recognize the fact that much can be accomplished for the work of our Boards through the agency of women.

---

[12] *Annual of the SBC* (1877): 7–8, 20–22; William W. Barnes, *The Southern Baptist Convention, 1845–1953* (Nashville: Broadman Press, 1954) 148.

Acting on this report, the convention called for two central committees in each state, one for home and one for foreign missions, to be appointed by the two boards. The plan called for the women's societies to report to the central committees and "these Committees to the Boards."[13]

The report of the Committee on Woman's Work at the meeting in 1879 offered evidence that the opposition to too much activity on the part of women was mounting. There was more evidence in 1881 when the convention recommended that the FMB, at its discretion, appoint "some competent woman superintendent" of the women's work to direct and promote the work and to act under the direction of the FMB. The board decided not to make such an appointment because "a false step now might entail fatal embarrassment for years to come." The following year the FMB proposed to "move slowly and cautiously" on the women's issue.[14] One can only wonder if Secretary Tupper had been put under pressure by some of the Southern Baptist brethren or had a vision of Southern Baptist women turning into women's rights activists.

By the late 1870s the SBC had come around to accepting women as playing an important part in missionary activity. At the same time, it was equally clear that women were to work with women and children and not to seek to preach to or teach men. In 1883 the Committee on Woman's Work reported, "One of the most hopeful features in the Missionary enterprise is the active part women are taking in the work [of foreign missions]." The report quickly added, "If our women become thoroughly

---

[13] *Annual of the SBC* (1877): 37; Barnes, *The Southern Baptist Convention*, 146.

[14] *Annual of the SBC* (1881): 22; *1882*, 54; Barnes, *The Southern Baptist Convention*, 146; Norman H. Letsinger, "The Status of Women in the Southern Baptist Convention in Historical Perspective," *Baptist History & Heritage* (January 1977): 39–40.

missionary in spirit they will train the children in that direction, and there will be more hope for the next generation."[15] Over and over again, it was emphasized that women's missionary work was to be limited to leading children and other women and *not* men.

All of the talk about utilizing the energies of women in the missionary enterprises of the SBC apparently encouraged women to step forward in 1884 when the convention was again held in Baltimore. There the first general meeting of Southern Baptist women was held. The "ladies in attendance" were regarded, however, as "chance visitors" who were not delegated by any "working body at home" to present reports or transact business. The women appeared again at the conventions of 1885 and 1886 and resolved to make their meeting a permanent part of the annual meeting of the SBC. The central committee in the state where the convention was to be held would plan their program each year.[16]

Obviously, there was nothing the leaders of the SBC could do about the women showing up in the convention city and holding a separate meeting. There was, however, plenty that they could do to prevent women from appearing on the floor of the convention, and they proved that in 1884 and 1885. When the FMB elected to exercise caution—no doubt from fear of causing an uproar among the brethren—and did not appoint a woman superintendent to oversee the work of the state central committees, a resolution was offered at the 1884 convention that the Home Mission Board (HMB) do it. Dr. J. William Jones, an elderly pastor from Virginia, opposed the resolution, believing it might be the "entering wedge for women's rights and women's speaking in public." The resolution provoked spirited debate and controversy. One "delegate" who favored the resolution argued that the women might "work without us, if we don't permit them

---

[15] *Annual of the SBC* (1883): 23–24.
[16] Barnes, *The Southern Baptist Convention*, 149.

to work with us." The opposition to a woman superintendent caused the matter to be referred by the convention to the HMB for consideration. That board took no action.[17]

The acrimony that emerged at the convention in 1884 carried over to the next year and was greatly intensified by the appearance of two women who sought to be seated as messengers at the 1885 annual meeting in Augusta, where the SBC had been founded forty years earlier. The two women were Mary Oldham (Mrs. J. P.) Eagle and Margaretta Dudgeon (Mrs. M. D.) Early of Arkansas. Mrs. Eagle's husband was president of the Arkansas Baptist Convention and soon-to-be governor of Arkansas. Because of the two Arkansas women, J. William Jones of Virginia "made a point of order, claiming ladies were not eligible to sit as members of the Convention." A committee of five was appointed to report on the right of women to be admitted. Jones was a member of the committee. In the majority report, three members said that they did not deem admission expedient, but they could find nothing in the body's constitution to prevent it. Jones and J. W. Kilpatrick of Georgia offered a minority report, which called for denial of admission to the two "female delegates" from Arkansas. Heated debate ensued over how the constitution should be interpreted.[18]

Speaking in favor of the minority report, Jones asserted, "For forty years the Convention has been in existence, and never yet has a female taken part in its deliberations." He was afraid, he said, that if the two ladies were seated, the convention "would be flooded with them next year." Others argued that women would take over the convention and occupy "the president's chair." J. B. Hawthorne of Alabama spoke up and

---

[17] *Annual of the SBC* (1884): 17; Fannie E. S. Heck, *In Royal Service: The Mission Work of Southern Baptist Women* (Richmond: Foreign Mission Board, 1913) 111–12; *Religious Herald* (15 May 1884) 3 and (22 May 1884) 2.

[18] Allen, *A Century to Celebrate*, 39; *Annual of the SBC* (1885): 13–14, 24, 30; appendix A, pp. III-IV; Barnes, *The Southern Baptist Convention*, 149–50.

insisted that if women were admitted as delegates, they could hold any office. Calling this revolutionary and wrong, Hawthorne contended that "our Southern women do not want it."[19]

Among those who was in favor of admitting the women was M. D. Early, the husband of one of the would-be messengers. He read the Arkansas report that stated, "The question before this Convention is, Shall the Baptist ladies of this country, who have sent more money into the vaults of this Convention than the men, be excluded from a part in its deliberation?" O. C. Pope, a pastor from Texas, called attention to the fact that twice before a woman had attended the convention as a messenger—Mrs. Myra E. Graves in 1877 and 1882.[20]

In the end the views of J. William Jones prevailed. Because of the hostility exhibited toward women's participation by male chauvinist members, the two Arkansas women withdrew their names as messengers. The convention voted 202 to 112 in favor of the minority report, but the matter did not end there. Because of the two women's withdrawal from serving as "delegates," the convention president ruled that the report could be withdrawn and not entered into the convention's minutes. Jones then pressed for a constitutional amendment to preclude women messengers from future conventions. By a vote of 131 to 42 the convention changed Article III of the SBC's constitution so that representation was to consist of "brethren" instead of "members." This meant that henceforth women were barred from going to the annual meetings as messengers. Not until 1918 would the ban against women messengers be overturned. Curiously, one woman expressed her complete satisfaction with the action taken at Augusta in 1885. She was Mrs. James Hime of Georgia, and she praised the decision to bar women messengers,

[19] Allen, *A Century to Celebrate*, 39; McBeth, "The Role of Women in Southern Baptist History," 13.

[20] Allen, *A Century to Celebrate*, 39; McBeth, "The Role of Women in Southern Baptist History," 12.

claiming it was men's duty to "see that no heads inferior to their own" should be permitted to supervise "the vast network of missions."[21]

The advances that women seemed to be making in the late 1870s and early 1880s were clearly a thing of the past after Augusta. Some of what happened at the 1885 convention was a reflection of what had already been happening in some state conventions. As women worked to organize on behalf of promoting missions, they sometimes encountered indifference and even outright opposition at the state and local levels. The Georgia Baptist Convention ignored reports sent to it concerning women's work. Pastors in Kentucky remained silent when approached for names of women in their churches who would be interested in organizing to promote missions. On some occasions the women were ridiculed, but women did have some support. When some men in Georgia argued that women were going to break up the churches, one pastor asserted that some of them needed to be broken up. In any event, Southern Baptist women were forced by what happened at the Augusta convention to do their work alone, and not a few of them resented it. Because of the action taken in 1885, men were excluded from the women's meetings, which were held in conjunction with, but apart from, the SBC's annual meetings.[22]

If women did want to drop into sessions of the annual conventions, they were compelled to sit in the visitors' gallery—in spite of the fact that a substantial majority of the SBC's one million members at that time were women. Even

---

[21] *Annual of the SBC* (1885): 13–14, 24, 30; appendix A, III-IV; Barnes, *The Southern Baptist Convention*, 150–51; McBeth, "The Role of Women in Southern Baptist History," 13; Ruth Tucker and Walter Liefield, *Daughters of the Church: Women in Ministry from New Testament Times to the Present* (Grand Rapids MI: Zondervan Publishing House, 1987) 284.

[22] Allen, *A Century to Celebrate*, 39; Heck, *In Royal Service*, 106–108, 114, 118–19.

though women bore their second-class status as SBC members with their usual forbearance, there is plenty of evidence to suggest that they were not happy about it. One woman wrote in the *Religious Herald* that men did not want them to meet in council with men and did not want them to meet in council with themselves. She added, "Did men want them to sit down and do nothing in God's cause, like so many of them [i.e., the men] have done for ages and are still doing?" Some women resented being confined to seats in the visitors' gallery and tried to go on the floor of the convention. On one occasion in 1899, when a woman attempted to go on the floor of the meeting, her attention was called to a "Delegates Only" sign on a post. An usher told her that the sign meant she could not enter the convention. She responded by saying that she understood the sign to mean that only delegates could climb the post! She also expressed the opinion that women ought to be allowed to take seats on the floor, in view of all the money women contributed to the convention boards.

Refusing to let women sit on the floor of the convention was not the end of the discrimination by the SBC. In 1892 the editor of the *Biblical Recorder* called on Southern Baptist churches in North Carolina to refuse the use of their buildings to all women speakers, no matter how good their cause. The editor objected to Baptist Young People's Training Union because young girls were allowed to speak in assemblies with teenage boys present. He insisted that there should be separate assemblies and that only boys should speak—even in the girls' assemblies. Also, opposition to allowing women messengers to be a part of annual meetings intensified. In 1894 there was an attempt to strengthen the ban against women messengers to the annual meeting by once again amending Article III so that it would read, "Representatives shall be male members in good standing with some regular Baptist church." A motion by W. H. Whitsitt of Southern Seminary to table the amendment was passed by a vote of 442 ayes to 142 nays.[23] Thus, the ban against women messengers remained, and the annual conventions still consisted of "brethren," instead of "male members." Apparently Whitsitt thought that specifying "male members" amounted to overkill.

While it is clear that most Southern Baptist men favored the subordinate position to which women had been assigned, it would be wrong to say that all of the brethren were male chauvinists. There were always some men around—even at the conventions—who wanted women to have more recognition and perhaps even equality. An indication of this is the 1895 report to the convention by the Committee on Woman's Work. It said:

> Many fears are expressed as to the doings of the uprising army of women workers. While many of us may not sympathize with these fears, the most conservative among us could not have asked these women to be more conservative and circumspect than they have been. Let us not charge against them the extravagances of others, but let their past record commend them as conserving every right tradition of our Convention.... The Southern Baptist Convention is stronger today because of the efforts of these consecrated women.

At least in part, the report's praise was aimed at the women who had formed the WMU seven years earlier. The WMU had male supporters who thought the organization was a good idea and others who supported it because they thought it would keep women from seeking leadership roles in the convention. Of

---

[23] Allen, *A Century to Celebrate*, 40, 303, 374; *Annual of the SBC* (1894): 13; McBeth, "The Role of Women in Southern Baptist History," 9, 13–14, 20–21.

course, a great many Southern Baptist brethren were contemptuous of the organization.[24]

The committee report's reference to "the extravagances of others" surely meant people like Elizabeth Cady Stanton, Susan B. Anthony, and Victoria Woodhull. Most Southern Baptists, including many Southern Baptist women, opposed the organized feminist movement and all efforts to bring about any significant change in the traditional role of women. Southern Baptist books spoke often and with few dissenting voices against women voting, speaking or preaching in mixed assemblies, and seeking an education alongside men. In spite of the inferior place assigned to women by Southern Baptist men, by this time the women were teaching most Sunday school classes (except classes of adult men, of course), carrying on most of the benevolent work, and promoting the mission program with little help from men. These things they continued to do patiently while men ran the churches. Only at the state level were any concessions made to women by the end of the nineteenth century and, then, not by all the state conventions. Most of the state conventions allowed them to serve as messengers, but not Alabama, Georgia, South Carolina, and Virginia. In a few instances women served on committees at the state level and even addressed their conventions.[25]

With the opening of the new century, the SBC appeared to be loosening up slightly with regard to where women sat at the annual conventions. Beginning in 1901 women were allowed to take seats on the floor of the convention, and in 1913 the convention heard directly, for the first time, a report from the

---

[24] *Annual of the SBC* (1895): 44; Jesse C. Fletcher, *The Southern Baptist Convention: A Sesquicentennial History* (Nashville: Broadman & Holman Publishers, 1994) 95.

[25] McBeth, "The Role of Women in Southern Baptist History," 9, 11–13, 16, 19: Rufus Spain, *At Ease in Zion: A Social History of Southern Baptists, 1865–1900* (Nashville: Vanderbilt University Press, 1961) 169–70.

WMU, but a man presented that report. Previously, the WMU had reported through the mission boards, but because 1913 was the organization's twenty-fifth anniversary, W. O. Carver recommended a direct report relative to that momentous event. The occasion contributed to improved relations between the SBC and the WMU, and thereafter women who wore their WMU badges were admitted to the floor of the convention. Women began attending annual conventions in increasing numbers because of their interest in denominational issues as well as to hear their own WMU report. Another step forward for women took place in 1916 when B. D. Gray, secretary of the Home Mission Board, allowed the WMU corresponding secretary, Kathleen Mallory, some of his time on the program. Thus, Miss Mallory became the first woman to speak to an SBC annual convention when she introduced Mrs. Maude R. McLure, who was the first principal of the WMU Training School that had been founded in 1907 for the purpose of training women missionaries. Miss Mallory and Mrs. McLure, who also spoke, were, according to the *Christian Index*, "smashing a custom that was 65 years old and maybe more." Some men, especially J. W. Porter, the editor of the *Western Recorder* who was as unflinchingly opposed to women speaking to men as he had ever been, were highly displeased by this concession to women, and the incident sparked a debate over women's rights. Speaking up against Porter and for women' rights was James B. Gambrell, editor of the *Baptist Standard*.[26]

Two years before B. D. Gray's gracious concession to the WMU at the 1916 convention, the first steps were taken toward allowing women the right not only to sit on the convention floor but to serve as messengers. In 1914 Robert H. Coleman of Dallas,

[26] Allen, *A Century to Celebrate*, 304, 306; Barnes, *The Southern Baptist Convention*, 165; Fletcher, *The Southern Baptist Convention*, 132; Alma Hunt, *History of Woman's Missionary Union* (Nashville: Convention Press, 1964) 83, 107.

Texas, began to push for removing the ban against women messengers. This sparked a debate that lasted for the next three years, but Coleman's proposal continued to gain support, and the appearance of Kathleen Mallory and Maude McLure before the convention in 1916 gave impetus to the cause, as did the report of the Committee on Woman's Work that same year. Read by W. C. James of Virginia, it said:

> The ministry of the women through the channels of the WMU is constructive—thoroughly so. Their object is to help all along the line of our denominational activities. There is not an enterprise of our Convention that is not loyally, enthusiastically, supported by the WMU, and we measure our words when we say that the pastor who ignores, or treats lightly or opposes the work of the Union, throws an impediment in the way of the gospel, endangers the success of his own ministry, and invites the displeasure of Almighty God—and this, not because the women are women, but because of the work which the women seek to do.[27]

Obviously some forward-looking men in the SBC were coming around to a more enlightened perspective on the women's issue, but, still, in 1917, when Robert Coleman presented his proposal to allow women to serve as messengers and vote on the business of the denomination, an acrimonious debate ensued. The convention that year was in New Orleans. Over a thousand women had gathered for the WMU meeting that was held in conjunction with, but apart from, the annual convention. They packed the galleries and applauded vigorously when the courageous gentleman from Texas offered his resolution, which

---

[27] *Annual of the SBC* (1916): 65; McBeth, "The Role of Women in Southern Baptist History," 14.

stated: "Whereas, women constitute so vital a part of the membership of our churches, both in numbers and workers; and, Whereas, The present wording of the Constitution of the Southern Baptist Convention is such as to prohibit the recognition of women as messengers; Therefore, be it *Resolved.* That Article III of the Constitution be so altered as to read as follows: Article III. The Convention shall consist (1) of messengers." Messengers was to replace the word "brethren."

After the bitter debate that followed Coleman's proposal, there was a strange turn of events. An attempt to table the resolution was defeated 324 to 242. President James B. Gambrell, who was sympathetic to the women's cause, surprisingly ruled that a constitutional change needed a two-thirds vote of "the total enrolled delegation," and not just a two-thirds vote of those present and voting. S. P. Brooks of Texas appealed the ruling, but the chair's ruling was sustained by a vote of 324 to 242. The resolution was then referred to a committee of five, with Coleman serving as chairman. It was the duty of the committee to study the resolution "for consideration and report next year."[28]

At the convention of 1918 Coleman's committee made its report, but only after some hesitation. Two of the committee members "had not been seen and a third did not agree to the report as it was prepared." Coleman was ready to ask that "the matter be dropped." The issue was about to be dropped until F. M. McConnell of Oklahoma called for a reading of the report. Very plainly the report recommended "the admission of women as messengers." McConnell argued that refusal to adopt the report would require, for the sake of consistency, excluding "women from our churches." He claimed that women had already been recognized by the Methodists and contended that Southern

---

[28] *Annual of the SBC* (1917): 37–38; Letsinger, "The Status of Women in the Southern Baptist Convention in Historical Perspective," 41; McBeth, "The Role of Women in Southern Baptist History," 14–15.

Baptists should follow suit. To committee chairman Coleman's surprise, the resolution passed overwhelmingly. Perhaps the easy passage of the resolution came, at least in part, because the SBC's action in 1917 had met with a highly unfavorable public response. The passage of the resolution in 1918 was most favorably received, prompting the editor of the *Religious Herald* to urge that women be given representation on every convention board, and the WMU thanked the brethren for now allowing women to sit as messengers. In order to prevent the kind of foot-dragging that had caused the resolution to be delayed a whole year, Coleman offered another resolution, which stated: "Article XIII. Any alteration which experience shall dictate may be made in these Articles by a vote of two-thirds of the members present when the vote is being taken without regard to total enrollment at any annual meeting of the Convention, provided, no amendment may be considered after the second day of the Convention." The resolution passed, thus making changes in the constitution possible by a vote of only two-thirds of those present and voting and not two-thirds of all messengers registered.[29]

At the 1919 annual meeting of the SBC many Southern Baptist women took advantage of their new status; many attended the convention as messengers from their churches. The Alabama delegation included 99 women out of 475, while Arkansas had 30 women in its delegation of 127. President Gambrell began his presidential address, "Brethren and Sisters of the Convention." Women consequently flocked to future conventions, and Gambrell became known as the "Baptist Commoner," for he endorsed woman's suffrage and lauded the victory of that movement in persuading Congress to pass the

---

[29] Allen, *A Century to Celebrate*, 307–308; *Annual of the SBC* (1918): 15, 18; *Christian Index* (23 May 1918) 3; Letsinger, "The Status of Women in the Southern Baptist Convention in Historical Perspective," 41; McBeth, "The Role of Women in Southern Baptist History," 15.

Nineteenth Amendment and to submit it to the states for ratification. There can be little doubt that there was a connection between the impending victory of the suffragists and the victory of Robert Coleman in securing messenger status for women at the 1919 meeting of the SBC. Given the general acquiescence of Southern Baptist women in their inferior status and the WMU's virtually ignoring the suffragist movement, Coleman's success was almost a miracle. While some Southern Baptist men like editors James B. Gambrell of the *Baptist Standard* and L. L. Gwaltney of the *Alabama Baptist* advocated woman's suffrage, as did Governor James B. Eagle of Arkansas, they represented a minority view among their brothers. It is curious that neither Gambrell's wife nor Gwaltney's openly advocated woman's suffrage in WMU circles.[30]

Thus, in spite of the fact that so few Southern Baptists fought for women's rights, there was a great leap forward in 1918 and 1919, thanks in part to the general movement for that cause. Those who thought that more victories were to be expected and that the opposition to advancing the cause of women could be expected to decline would presently find that most Southern Baptist men were convinced that sufficient concessions had already been made. Amazingly, as far as the majority of them was concerned, Southern Baptist women agreed. Women certainly became more active, but only a few pushed for additional recognition and status. They did not move into leadership roles. Only one or two served on boards during the 1920s, and during the years 1927 to 1958 only five women served on the SBC's powerful Executive Committee. In the early 1920s the WMU did request that more women be placed on the Executive Committee and the boards, but that request was obviously not honored. For years the percentage of women

---

[30] Allen, *A Century to Celebrate*, 235–37, 307–308; McBeth, "The Role of Women in Southern Baptist History," 15.

serving on all convention agencies and boards was 5 percent or
less of the total number serving. Not until the 1960s and 1970s
would women be elected as vice presidents of the convention and
then against some opposition. Never has a woman been elected
president of the SBC.[31]

The 1920s brought a few small victories to women, culmi-
nating in an address to the annual convention by the WMU
president in 1929. Before that happened, another WMU
president, Minnie Kennedy (Mrs. W. C.) James of Texas asserted
herself in 1922 by letting the SBC know about her frustration
over male domination of the convention. It was said that she had
the "mind of a man and the emotions of a woman," and she pas-
sionately made the case for equal and fair treatment of women.
She wrote, "Up to this good hour women have had but little share
in the administration of the affairs of the denomination. It has
been ours in many cases to inaugurate a plan and then have it
taken up by the denomination at large and carried on." As a
result of her efforts, the 1922 convention passed a motion by a
vote of 1,151 to 615 to give equal consideration to women.
What followed was discouraging; a few women went on the
boards, and none went on the Executive Committee. The next
year, however, Willie Turner Dawson became the first woman
ever to be nominated for an SBC office. She was nominated for
vice president. Four vice presidents were elected, but Turner was
not one of them. Not until 1963 would another woman be
nominated for vice president. She was Marie Mathis, the WMU
president, and she won the SBC office of second vice president.
Her election was not applauded by all, however, and it would be
ten more years before another woman would be nominated for
second vice president.[32]

---

[31] Hunt, *History of Woman's Missionary Union*, 108–109; McBeth, "The
Role of Women in Southern Baptist History," 15–25.

[32] Allen, *A Century to Celebrate*, 311; Hunt, *History of Woman's
Missionary Union*, 109–10.

If Southern Baptist women had not organized and formed their WMU, it is likely that not a single woman would have served on an SBC board until after World War II, for all the women who were elevated to positions on boards and committees were WMU leaders—most of them being state WMU presidents. This was true until the 1980s. In the minds of some, a breakthrough for women came in 1928 when the SBC invited Ethelene Boone (Mrs. W. J.) Cox, then president of the WMU, to speak about her organization at the convention in 1929. There was no recorded opposition, but controversy emerged during the months that followed. The General Association of Kentucky, led by that scourge of women, J. W. Porter, passed a resolution against women addressing a mixed assembly. He contended that allowing women to speak to men in assembly would violate biblical teaching and 1,900 years of historical precedent. The issue was raised and debated in several state Baptist journals and at a number of pastors' meetings. All of this was apparently done to prevent Cox from addressing the 1929 convention, but it failed to work. Before she was scheduled to speak on that occasion in Memphis, Porter was on hand with his resolution from the General Association of Kentucky, protesting against "the president of the WMU or any other woman addressing this Convention." He insisted that it was "unscriptural for a woman to address this body." "This is a gesture to please the women and get more money," Porter shouted. "We should not trade God for gold nor Christ for cash." M. E. Dodd, a pastor from Shreveport, Louisiana, replied to Porter's contentions by saying that "in Christ there is neither male nor female" and "we are one in Christ." When the Kentucky editor's resolution was voted down by an avalanche of "noes," he picked up his hat and left the meeting hall.[33]

---

[33] Allen, *A Century to Celebrate*, 312; *Annual of the SBC* (1929): 102; Paper by Charles DeWeese, Baptist History Files, Women's Role in Church. Southern Baptist Historical Library and Archives, Nashville, TN, 13–14; Hunt,

Following the commotion precipitated by Porter's obstructionist effort, George W. Truett, highly respected pastor of First Baptist Church in Dallas, Texas, introduced Ethelene Boone Cox and bade the convention to "hear this gentlewoman." This gentlewoman, tall and beautiful with a strong melodious voice, made an impressive appearance. According to an article in the *Memphis Press-Scimitar*, there was "no bitterness in Mrs. Cox's address," and she "pleaded for a greater missionary program in the interest of world peace as well as Christianity." She asked that women be given the opportunity "for unlimited expression in the work of missions." The *Annual of the SBC* for 1929 notes that Mrs. Cox addressed the convention, but what she said was not recorded on its pages.[34]

Although Mrs. Cox apparently hurled no barbs at the anti-woman element in the SBC on that occasion, she was not entirely free of resentment. When asked what she thought of J. W. Porter's attempt to bar her from speaking, she reportedly said:

No woman went to sleep in the garden. No woman denied Him. No woman betrayed Him. But it was a woman, acting on intuition who tried to save Him.

It was the women who followed Him to Calvary and wept for Him. It was the women who made the last offering to Him. It was the women who stood by and refused to leave as He hung on the cross. It was the women who were at the tomb.[35]

History of Woman's Missionary Union, 110, 115–20; McBeth, *Women in Baptist Life*, 119–20; *Religious Herald* (16 May 1929) 3.

[34] *Annual of the SBC* (1929): 48; DeWeese Paper, Baptist History Files, 13–14; Hunt, *History of Woman's Missionary Union*, 115.

[35] DeWeese Paper, SBHLA, 13–14. DeWeese's source is an article that appeared in the *Memphis Press-Scimitar*.

Mrs. Cox was president of the WMU, but the report of the convention's WMU committee had been read to the convention before she spoke—by a man, Finley F. Gibson of Kentucky. The tradition of men giving the WMU report was still in place, and this could not have pleased her. Nine years later, however, Mrs. Cox, then WMU treasurer instead of president, did present the organization's report, and Mrs. F. W. Armstrong, then president of the WMU, addressed the annual meeting.[36]

Women, all of whom were officers in the WMU, began to have a more visible place in conventions, and several WMU presidents actually addressed conventions; seemingly this would mean a steady rise in the status of women in the SBC. Such was not the case. Women's efforts continued to go largely unheralded. Not much happened to give women increased visibility and recognition after Ethelene Boone Cox's breakthrough address to the annual meeting in 1929 and her presentation of the WMU annual report in 1938. Women remained in the shadows of the denomination and still did not move into leadership roles. This began to change in the mid-1950s as more women attended the annual conventions as messengers. In 1968 about a third of the messengers at the convention were women, while in 1978 the number rose to 42 percent. Some enlightened Southern Baptist brothers even began to push for women in high office. In 1972 Russell Dilday, an Atlanta pastor, nominated WMU president Marie Mathis, former second vice president of the convention, for the presidency of the SBC. She did not make the runoff. Still, there were signs that women were at last gaining some recognition. Myra Gray Bates, wife of Charlotte pastor Carl Bates, became the first woman to make a nominating speech at an annual convention in 1975. The following year she was elected second vice president, and in 1981 WMU president Christine Burton Gregory of Virginia was elected

---

[36] McBeth, *Women in Baptist Life*, 120.

first vice president. By 1983 women had about 10 percent of the SBC's committee assignments, but the brakes were already being applied to women's increased participation and representation. The SBC was slowly falling into the grasp of the denomination's fundamentalist element, and fundamentalist presidents Bailey Smith and Charles Stanley thwarted further efforts to promote the cause of Southern Baptist sisters.[37]

Obtaining even the little recognition that came to women in the 1960s and 1970s had been very difficult and came about in an atmosphere of tension and opposition. Marie Mathis's election as second vice president of the convention in 1963 prompted Richard Batchelder, a messenger from Kansas, to introduce a motion to amend the denomination's constitution. He wanted Article V, Section 2 changed so that convention officers would be limited to the male sex. The chair ruled the motion out of order, declaring that no amendment could be introduced to the convention after the sessions of the second day.[38]

The Women's Lib movement no doubt influenced some Southern Baptist women, and men, to press for enhanced status for women, but, as always, it also prompted Southern Baptist conservatives, men and some women, to stiffen their resistance and insist on maintaining the old traditions. At several conventions in the 1970s Mrs. Richard Sappington of Houston introduced resolutions specifically condemning Women's Lib, as she did in 1972 and again in 1974. The latter year in particular produced a huge controversy, largely because the denomination's Christian Life Commission (CLC), probably made aware by the Women's Lib movement of women's second-class status in American society, offered a resolution that provoked conservatives as they had not been provoked in a long while. The CLC recommended a change in the bylaws so that at least one-

---

[37] Allen, *A Century to Celebrate*, 310–11, 313.
[38] *Annual of the SBC* (1963): 79.

fifth of all convention boards and committees would consist of women. Noting that "injustice toward women persists to some degree in every institution in society," the recommendation read in part, "That we work to develop greater sensitivity to both overt and covert discrimination against women and that we endeavor through religious, political, social, business and educational structures to eliminate such discrimination." And, "That our churches and our denominational agencies bear witness to the rest of society by rejecting discrimination against women." Mrs. Sappington rose to challenge the recommendation and to spew out more arguments for women's submission. She insisted that women should not speak out, but accept their traditional roles. Another messenger from Texas moved that the convention go on record as opposing the endorsement of women as chaplains. As it turned out, the 1974 convention did nothing to advance the cause of women. A constitutional amendment offered by Tom Reynolds, a pastor from Lubbock, Texas, would have excluded ordination of women in Southern Baptist churches. Only men should be ministers, Reynolds contended. After the fact, the *Baptist Standard* reported, "The explosive issue of ordination of women was handed back to local churches last week by messengers of the Southern Baptist Convention." After Mrs. Sappington warned that a positive vote on the report "could revolutionize our denomination" and Cecil Sherman, chairman of the commission, observed that women composed 55 percent of the denomination's membership but only 5 percent of its boards, the convention voted to table Reynolds's proposal as well as the CLC's report on "Freedom of Women."[39]

The obvious bias demonstrated against women by the 1974 convention provoked considerable debate during that summer. Many letters to the editor appeared in Baptist journals. Not all

---

[39] *Annual of the SBC* (1973): 87, and (1974): 63, 73, 79, 209; *Baptist Standard* (29 May 1974) 8 and (19 June 1974) 4; McBeth, "The Role of Women in Southern Baptist History," 24–25.

Southern Baptist women were submissive in the fashion that Mrs. Sappington thought proper. Generally speaking, the women who expressed themselves in letters thought it would be worthwhile for women to be involved in leadership roles, while Southern Baptist men generally opposed such a change. Invariably the men who wrote letters quoted scriptures that admonished women to remain silent in the churches. One writer of the post-World War II period had referred to citing these scriptures as "The St. Paul Hang-up." Those who deplored this "hang-up" claimed that the Apostle Paul's restrictions on women should be viewed the same way as Paul's views on slavery—that is, addressed only to the culture of his time. Advocates of this position further maintained that the church should purge itself of "The St. Paul Hang-up."[40]

With the Women's Lib movement demanding greater rights for women and with the 1973 highly controversial *Roe v. Wade* decision on abortion recently imposed on American society by the US Supreme Court, the national atmosphere and, especially, the atmosphere in Southern Baptist circles, were saturated with reactionary sentiments during the mid-to-late 1970s. There were those who kept trying to move forward to secure additional rights for women, and there were others who were determined to stop them. Still others just sat tight and hoped the social storm would blow over and not provoke violence. That some Southern Baptist women would push forward was indicated by the 1978 Consultation of Women in Church Related Vocations, which was mentioned earlier. At that gathering, women who felt a sense of call, but also felt isolated, had the opportunity to talk to other women in similar circumstances. Within five years the group of women at that meeting, along with others, would evolve into Southern Baptist Women in Ministry and sponsor a publication called *Folio*. In the year of the Consultation a survey of women

---

[40] *The Baptist Program* (January 1975): 22–23; McBeth, "The Role of Women in Southern Baptist History," 21–22.

employees of the SBC showed that only a minority of the women surveyed felt that the SBC was unfair to women employees. Still, there was evidence that most Southern Baptists were doing little to advance the cause of women. Another survey, one conducted during 1978 in North Carolina by Charles V. Petty, executive director of the Christian Life Council of the North Carolina Baptist Convention, revealed that fifty-seven associations had taken no stand on the role of women in churches, while two had voted *for* leadership roles for women and one *against* such roles. Only 128 churches had ordained women deacons, while twelve associations reported that some of their churches had ordained women ministers—eighteen in total.[41]

With little or no encouragement from men in the SBC, some strong-minded women continued to promote their cause. Other denominations had already taken forward steps, but Southern Baptists, at least for the most part, either resisted or did nothing. Professor Sarah Frances Anders of Louisiana College delivered an address at New Orleans in 1982 in which she noted that other denominations had been moving for over a dozen years to allow women to enjoy leadership roles, while the SBC lagged behind. She proclaimed, "Other denominations are now more open to women in the pastorate than Southern Baptists are." She argued that 80 percent of American Baptist-ordained women were serving as pastors; 73 percent of Lutherans were; 62 percent of Presbyterians were; and 50 percent of Disciples of Christ were. In contrast, less than a dozen women in the whole SBC held pastorates.[42]

---

[41] "Survey of Women Employees of Southern Baptist Convention Agencies, April–May, 1978," Baptist History Files, Women Employees, SBC, Southern Baptist Historical Library and Archives, Nashville, TN, 9; Leon McBeth, *The Baptist Heritage* (Nashville: Broadman Press, 1987) 693; McBeth, *Women in Baptist Life*, 178–79.

[42] Sarah Frances Anders, "Women in Ministry: The Distaff of the Church in Action" (An address delivered in New Orleans in 1982) Baptist History Files,

It was no wonder that some Southern Baptists cringed at the thought of women becoming ministers, for some of the assertive women were taking positions that most considered radical. For instance, some women claimed that God showed no gender favorites in any of the Gospels and that God's person could include two genders. God, they claimed, is "androgynous" or "gender transcendent." Moreover, they argued that Southern Baptists could widen their concept of God by praying "in the name of the Father and Mother." They insisted that both men and women were called to service by God on an equal basis, for all persons bear the image of God. Jesus, they contended, accepted women and gave all of his followers the same gifts of ministry with no regard to gender.[43] Such views went much too far for most conservative Southern Baptists and especially for Southern Baptist fundamentalists who were well on their way to gaining control of the SBC by the mid-1980s. Indeed, the forces of reaction were working to overturn liberal gains on all fronts. On the political front, for example, Republicans had succeeded in electing Ronald Reagan as President of the United States in 1980. In politics, religion, and society the progressive gains realized in the 1960s and 1970s were being erased during the reactionary decade of the 1980s. It was done for a dozen years with the blessings of the nation's highest elected officials, Presidents Ronald Reagan and George Bush. Women's issues were ignored and women's efforts to enhance their status were opposed at many levels and in many segments of society.

To throw up a gigantic roadblock in the way of women who were pushing for enhanced status obviously became an objective of the fundamentalists who were steadily taking control of the SBC. Resolution No. 3, which was adopted at the 1984 convention in Kansas City, made this crystal clear. Not only was

---

Women in Ministry Group, Southern Baptist Historical Library and Archives, Nashville, TN. 4.

[43] Paper by Carl Kell, Baptist History Files, Women in Ministry, 3–6, 8–9.

the resolution anti-woman, it was also against social and religious change of all sorts. It read:

> WHEREAS, While Paul commends women and men alike in other roles of ministry and service (Titus 2:1-10), he excludes women from pastoral leadership (I Tim. 2:12) to preserve a submission to God required because the man was first in creation and the woman was first in the Edenic fall (I. Tim. 2:13ff).
>
> Therefore, be it *Resolved*. That we not decide concerns of Christian doctrine and practice by modern cultural, sociological, and ecclesiastical trends or by emotional factors: that we remind ourselves of the dearly bought Baptist principle of the final authority of Scripture in matters of faith and conduct; and that we encourage the service of women in all aspects of church life and work other than pastoral functions and leadership roles entailing ordination.[44]

The carefully crafted language of this resolution did not obscure the fact that those who drafted it blamed women for the fall of the human race and reasserted the long-held view of Southern Baptist men that women should stay out of the pulpit.

The following year saw the forced resignation of Howard Bramlette, an editor for the Sunday School Board. Two articles that he allowed to be published in *The Baptist Student* cost him his job. The first was an article on the roles of women in Southern Baptist life, while the second, coming a few months later, was critical of mixing right-wing politics and religion.[45] Since fundamentalists were ascending quickly to power, they took steps to put pressure on editors of Baptist publications, if those

---

[44] *Annual of the SBC* (1984): 65.
[45] Fletcher, *The Southern Baptist Convention*, 293.

editors held or allowed the publication of contrary views on political and social issues and particularly women's issues. This trend would continue and cause a huge flap in 1990 when Al Shackleford and Dan Martin, the director and news editor respectively of Baptist Press, were fired in an atmosphere of high drama.

Once the fundamentalists were firmly in control, which they were by 1990, women were virtually removed from any visibility in the SBC. The only time the new leaders of the Convention turned their attention to women, it was to place restrictions on them. Even before 1990, fundamentalist Southern Baptists had made their influence felt at the annual conventions at which they consistently elected presidents who saw eye to eye with them. They sponsored and secured adoption of two pro-life resolutions in the 1980s, thus changing the Convention's former position, which had allowed for abortion in the event of rape or incest or to save the life of the mother. In some states Baptist associations withdrew fellowship from churches that ordained women as deacons and ministers.[46]

One highly publicized example of what might happen to a woman who dared to take on a Southern Baptist pastorate, as well as the consequences for the church that called her, was the case of Nancy Sehested. In 1987 Mrs. Sehested was appointed pastor of Prescott Memorial Baptist Church, a small church in Memphis, Tennessee. In the same city Adrian Rogers, fundamentalist president of the SBC, was pastor of the huge Bellevue Baptist Church. The Shelby Baptist Association, in which both churches held membership, decided that Sehested's appointment by Prescott Memorial was unacceptable, in spite of the fact that Sehested had been an associate pastor in Georgia and came from a line of Baptist ministers in Texas. She was the

---

[46] David T. Morgan, *The New Crusades, the New Holy Land: Conflict in the Southern Baptist Convention, 1969–1991* (Tuscaloosa and London: University of Alabama Press, 1996) 152–57.

daughter and granddaughter of Baptist pastors. Her impressive Baptist connections meant nothing to the Shelby Baptist Association, which proceeded to disfellowship Prescott Memorial and, incredibly, to defend doing so by arguing that Eve's behavior in the Garden of Eden had made women ineligible to lead congregations![47] Ultimately, Sehested gave up on serving as a Baptist pastor, believing that even the moderate Baptists, who had fought the fundamentalists for control of the SBC and lost, did not want women in the pulpit. In the year 2000, having abandoned the pastorate, Sehested was quoted as saying, "The moderates might as well have a statement against women pastors. Even in moderate churches where they say they're open to women pastors, it's still difficult. The doors are just not open. For those of us who have been on this road a long time, we've realized it's a lot more difficult to change deeply ingrained traditions than we ever imagined." When she spoke those words, Sehested had become a prison chaplain in North Carolina.[48]

The lessons that Sehested learned between 1987 and 2000 were learned by many other Baptists—men as well as women. The men who cared about women's issues, at least for the most part, stopped attending the annual conventions. Many moderate Baptist churches remained in the SBC but mainly supported quasi-denominations like the Cooperative Baptist Fellowship and the Alliance of Baptists. An increasing number of churches formally withdrew from the SBC. The withdrawal of those men and women who favored enhancing the status of women meant that the fundamentalists had virtually all the votes of the messengers who attended the annual meetings and could propose and adopt any resolutions they desired. And they did. Excluding women from the pastorate was not nearly enough for some of them. In 1998 they added a "family amendment" to the Baptist Faith and

---

[47] Ibid., 156.

[48] Greg Garrison, "Baptists to Argue Women's Roles," *Birmingham News* (11 June 2000) 15A–16A.

Message Statement of 1963 that called for submission of wives to their husbands, stating, "The husband and wife are of equal worth before God, since both are created in God's image.... A wife is to submit herself graciously to the servant leadership of her husband even as the church willingly submits to the headship of Christ." The statement went on to say that a wife was to "respect" her husband, serve as his "helper," manage the household, and "nurture the next generation." These were statements that a convention held in *1898*, or even in *1848*, might have proposed and embraced with considerable enthusiasm. It is interesting that Dorothy Patterson, wife of fundamentalist SBC president Paige Patterson; Mary K. Mohler, wife of fundamentalist Southern Seminary president Al Mohler; and Richard Land, fundamentalist director of the SBC's Christian Life Commission, all served on the committee that offered the proposed changes to the Baptist Faith and Message Statement of 1963. Messenger Tim Owings of Georgia attempted to amend the committee's report, but he was voted down after Dorothy Patterson and former SBC fundamentalist president Adrian Rogers spoke against amending it.[49]

During the months leading up to the 2000 convention, Adrian Rogers served as chairman of a committee that wrote and proposed what was essentially a new Baptist Faith and Message Statement. Once adopted, it was to supersede the 1963 Statement as the SBC's confession of faith. The report was released and publicized widely in convention circles on 18 May presumably to inform messengers ahead of time and limit the time needed to discuss the alterations at the upcoming annual meeting. Immediately the document provoked controversy on such issues as soul competency, priesthood of believers, and—to a lesser extent—women pastors. The 2000 statement included the words, "While both men and women are gifted for service in the church,

---

[49] *Annual of the SBC* (1998): 78, 81–82.

the office of pastor is limited to men as qualified by Scripture."[50] Shortly before the annual convention, the Rogers committee released a statement explaining the report. In the matter of women pastors, the explanation said, "First, we faced the fact that the Bible is clear in presenting the office of pastor as restricted to men. There is no biblical precedent for a woman in the pastorate, and the Bible teaches that women should not teach in authority over men.... Other denominations are abandoning biblical teaching and calling women to serve as pastors." At the convention, only thirty minutes were allotted to discuss the new version of the Baptist Faith and Message Statement. The time for deliberation was extended, but there was no discussion on the issue of women pastors, since all of the discussion time was consumed by debate over soul competency and priesthood of believers. A few amendments were made, but for the most part, the recommendations of the committee were overwhelmingly approved. The newly elected president who was chosen to succeed Paige Patterson was James Merritt, the forty-seven-year-old pastor of the First Baptist Church of Snellville, Georgia. Merritt praised the work of the committee and was quoted as saying, "The scripture makes it very plain without any apology that the calling of God into the ministry...is for men only."[51] Merritt's statement and the action taken by the messengers at the 2000 convention offered clear indication that the specter of J. W. Porter still hovered ominously over the annual meetings of the SBC.

In view of the fact that the National Council of Churches has had women in leadership roles since its founding in 1950 and since most mainline Protestant denominations have moved gradually toward allowing women a more active role in guiding the destinies of their churches, the attitude and actions of the

---

[50] Garrison, "Baptists to Argue Women's Roles," 15A–16A.

[51] *Alabama Baptist* (8 June 2000) 5 and (22 June 2000) 1–2; *Atlanta Constitution,* Academic Universe Document 1 (14 June 2000) 1.

SBC in regard to women during the closing decades of the twentieth century was nothing short of astonishing. In June 2000 the Southern Baptist Convention took a long leap backward into the nineteenth century, and Southern Baptist women found themselves back where they had been for most of the time since the founding of the SBC in 1845—in search of status. And the prospects for finding it looked very dim indeed.

CHAPTER 4

"THE PERISHING MILLIONS OF CHINA"

SOUTHERN BAPTIST WOMEN MISSIONARIES: IN SEARCH OF SELF-FULFILLMENT

In the fifth decade of the nineteenth century Baptists of the South were passionate about many things, missions and slaves among them. After all, Christ himself had commanded his followers to go into all the world and win converts, and the Apostle Paul, the first great missionary of Christianity, had condoned slavery. Since both missions and slavery were biblical, the Baptists of the South saw nothing wrong with missionaries being slave-owners. Their more morally sensitive Baptist brethren in the North did, however, and by the 1840s the Triennial Convention, which was composed of Baptist churches from both regions, concluded that slave-owners should be precluded from serving as missionaries. Hence the 1845 meeting in Augusta, Georgia and the founding of the Southern Baptist Convention. Baptists in the South were determined both to carry out the Great Commission and to keep their slaves.

As far as commitment to missions was concerned, the fledgling SBC demonstrated that by the creation immediately of two boards—a board to promote foreign missions and another to further domestic missions. From the very beginning of the new convention women showed a deep interest in missions, but outside of giving their money for the cause, most women could not participate directly in the mission enterprise. Exceptions were the women who accompanied their husband missionaries to the mission fields. The first great Southern Baptist mission field was China, apparently because it was the most populous nation on earth and offered the prospect of millions of converts to the Christian faith from among the many "benighted" heathen Chinese. Eventually Southern Baptists would branch out and send missionaries to other countries, but for a long time their greatest efforts were made on behalf of China, and numerous Southern Baptist women committed their lives to the work there. Lottie Moon's name looms largest among them, of course, but there were other great women—Martha Foster Crawford and Willie Kelly to name but two—who were also profoundly committed to winning the Chinese to Christ. These three and others of lesser fame were often frustrated because the male missionaries in the field and the Foreign Mission Board imposed the same inferior status on them that the SBC assigned to women back home. The struggles of women missionaries at home and abroad reveal much about the attitude of Southern Baptists toward women.

Baptist missionaries were in China before the Southern Baptist Convention was established in 1845. Jehu Lewis Shuck, who would later serve as a Southern Baptist missionary, and his wife, Henrietta Hall Shuck, went there in 1836, and Mrs. Shuck enjoys the distinction of being the first American Protestant woman to arrive in China as a missionary. She died there prior to the founding of the SBC. Unlike the Triennial Convention from which SBC members had withdrawn, the new denomination announced a policy of declining to send unmarried women to a mission field. That changed in 1849 when the SBC Foreign Mission Board decided to experiment by appointing Harriet A. Baker, a single woman from Powhatan County, Virginia, as a missionary to Canton, China. Her appointment was announced on 5 March 1849, at a time when American, and especially Southern women, were assigned to a role similar to that of children. They were to be seen and not heard, in spite of the fact that some American women had sounded the tocsin of social revolution at Seneca Falls the year before.[1]

Harriet Baker was thrilled at the prospect of reaching "the benighted millions of China," she said in a letter to James Taylor, corresponding secretary of the Foreign Mission Board. Shortly before her appointment she wrote Taylor to say that she had despaired of going to a foreign land and had decided to go to Texas as a school teacher, but it was the "greatest desire of her heart" to serve as a missionary, "if the board would deem me worthy." Less than a month later, her appointment was made, but it was not until March 1850 that she was on her way to Canton to open a girls' school. She arrived there in July. By the end of the year, because of certain "difficulties," she left Canton and headed for Shanghai. Her main difficulty, it appears, was with another missionary, Issachar J. Roberts. Baker had traveled to Canton with Roberts and his second wife, Virginia Young Roberts, a woman who would prove to be mentally unstable. Roberts appears to have been incorrigible and sought to control Baker's work. She wrote on 24 December 1850 to Archibald Thomas of Richmond, "Mr. Roberts will let me have only $6 per month for

---

[1] Catherine B. Allen, *A Century to Celebrate: History of Woman's Missionary Union* (Birmingham AL: Woman's Missionary Union, 1987) 18; Letters to James Taylor, Lucy Nichols, and Archibald Thomas, 1849–1850, Harriet A. Baker File, Southern Baptist Historical Library and Archives, Nashville, TN; William R. Estep, *Whole Gospel, Whole World: The Foreign Mission Board of the Southern Bapitist Convention, 1845–1995* (Nashville: Broadman & Holman Publishers, 1995) 119.

a teacher. I cannot get a good one for less than $8." Roberts was just as unhappy with Baker as she was with him, accusing her of circulating "an evil report" about him. Besides Baker's troubles with other missionaries—especially Roberts—she soon had health problems, and at the end of 1853 she resigned and went home. Her unfortunate, short-lived experience in China prompted the FMB to discontinue sending single women missionaries for nearly twenty years. After all, the experiment had been undertaken with some hesitation because it was in conflict with contemporary societal and denominational attitudes toward women. The FMB apparently decided that other voices in the convention and society had been right and its board members wrong: the experiment was a failure that should not be repeated.[2]

This attitude prevailed until 1872, when Edmonia Moon, the younger sister of the famous Lottie Moon, was allowed to go to China by the FMB as a self-supporting missionary, and Lula Whilden was permitted to go along with her married sister, Jumille Williams and her husband, Nicholas B. Williams. The fact that "Eddie" Moon was willing to support herself appealed to the FMB, which found itself short on funds. Both Eddie and Lottie Moon were drawn to an interest in China through their correspondence with Martha Crawford, who had gone there with her husband Tarleton Perry ("T. P.") Crawford in 1852. Upon her arrival in China, Eddie moved in with the Crawfords and began a correspondence with Lottie that would result in the latter's sailing for China in 1873. T. P. Crawford, writing from China and probably encouraged by Eddie, urged the FMB to appoint Lottie, which it did on 7 July 1873. She was to be supported by women of several churches who had organized missionary societies. Neither the Moon sisters nor Lula Whilden

---

[2] Allen, *A Century to Celebrate*, 174; *Annual of the SBC* (1849): 49 and (1855): 73–89 passim; Estep, *Whole Gospel, Whole World*, 119–20; Letters to James Taylor, Lucy Nichols, and Archibald Thomas, Harriet A. Baker File, SBHLA.

could have gone to China had not Henry A. Tupper, the new corresponding secretary of the FMB in 1872, prevailed upon the board to abandon its policy of no-single-women-need-apply.[3]

The 1872 annual meeting of the SBC gave denominational approval to the FMB's new policy of allowing single women to be appointed as missionaries. The report of the Committee on Bible Women was submitted and read by J. W. M. Williams of Maryland. It endorsed "the policy of the [Foreign Mission] Board in sending unmarried women, who have consecrated their lives to the work of mission[s], into the foreign field." The report also encouraged the organization of "Female Missionary Societies" in churches by having "pious women" assemble the sisters and organize them for the purpose of "cultivating the missionary spirit and systematic contributions." In commenting on the new policy, the *Western Recorder* offered a rather backhanded endorsement, saying, " Our Foreign Mission Board has decided, very properly, to send ummarried women, in connection with our missionaries, to labor for their own sex in heathen lands.... We predict that, kept within her proper sphere, woman will be a most valuable auxiliary in the work of spreading the gospel. Why shouldn't she? Didn't she have much to do in bringing the curse upon the race? And ought she not to do all she can to remove it?"[4]

Even though some in the denomination could not help but disdain women while awkwardly trying to compliment them, at least the FMB seemed to be excited about its mission work in general and the efforts of women in particular. It was noted in the FMB report that "Sisters Whilden and Moon expect to sail

---

[3] Allen, *A Century to Celebrate*, 174; Estep, *Whole Gospel, Whole World*, 119–120; Wayne Flynt and Gerald Berkley, *Taking Christianity to China: Alabama Missionaries in the Middle Kingdom, 1850–1950* (Tuscaloosa and London: University of Alabama Press, 1997) 198–99; Alma Hunt, *History of Woman's Missionary Union* (Nashville: Convention Press, 1964) 13–14.

[4] *Annual of the SBC* (1872): 35; *Western Recorder*, 18 May 1872, 2.

from San Francisco on the 1st of May, for their several fields in China." Eddie Moon was to join the mission at Tengchow while "Sister Williams and Miss Whilden will join the Canton Mission." The report further noted that "women societies are organizing to support Bible-women at our Missionary stations."[5]

Although it would not be known for decades to come, Southern Baptist mission efforts in China were destined to be revolutionized when that diminutive woman from Virginia—Lottie Moon—arrived in that land. She did not overturn tradition suddenly or with great fanfare. She did it gradually and quietly by being and doing, at least for the most part, what was expected of a single woman on the mission field. Amidst political infighting among missionaries Jesse B. Hartwell and T. P. Crawford and political skirmishes between Crawford and the FMB, Lottie Moon carried on her work in the manner she believed God wanted her to do it. Catherine B. Allen, her biographer, justifiably calls her "the most famous of all Southern Baptists past and present."

Mission activity in China was not invented by Lottie Moon; it had been carried on for decades before her arrival there. J. L. Shuck was a missionary in China before the advent of the SBC and then later served as a missionary appointed by the SBC. He lost two wives while serving in China. His first wife, Henrietta Hall Shuck, had devoted herself to learning Chinese so that she might better serve the mission. After her death, Shuck married Eliza Sexton, who died in childbirth during 1851. She used her house for a chapel and invited Chinese women to participate in services on Friday afternoons. Shuck called both of his deceased wives the "noblest of women, which God in kindness gave for a little while on earth to this unworthy servant." Another missionary, Matthew T. Yates, said of Eliza Shuck: "She was devoted to the interest of her husband and family as well as the

[5] *Annual of the SBC* (1872): 42.

best interest of the mission." Other women who were with their husbands in China during the 1840s were Mrs. T. W. Tobey, Mrs. J. S. James, and Mrs. M. T. Yates. Unfortunately, Mrs. James would die by drowning in 1849 along with her husband, when the vessel on which they were sailing from Canton to Hong Kong sank "within sight of Hong Kong." According to the FMB's 1849 annual report, the Jameses were "unexpectedly ushered into the presence of God." The Jameses, along with the others mentioned above, were part of the Shanghai mission. In 1849, the same year in which the Jameses were lost, Mrs. Tobey became ill and had to return to the United States.[6]

Missionaries appointed to Canton in 1849 included Mr. and Mrs. George Pearcy, Mr. and Mrs. B. W. Whilden, and Miss Harriet Baker. The convention was hopeful that Chinese women could be reached, noting that a building called the Leen Heng Ki chapel would seat one hundred people and that it had "a room suitably arranged for females whenever we shall have a female missionary or two with whom other females may assemble." A big problem at Canton was I. J. Roberts, who seemed to keep the mission in turmoil. He just could not get along with the other missionaries, particularly "Miss Baker and Mr. Bridgman." As indicated earlier, Baker eventually left for Shanghai and ultimately for home, and Bridgman committed suicide by slitting his throat. Roberts was investigated by the FMB, and his dismissal was recommended.[7]

Arriving amidst the tension-filled atmosphere surrounding the Shanghai mission in 1852 were the Crawfords, whose impact on Baptist mission work in China was second only to that of

---

[6] Allen, *The New Lottie Moon Story* (Nashville: Broadman Press, 1980), foreword; *Annual of the SBC* (1849): 52; Paper by Charles DeWeese, Baptist History Files, Women's Role in Church. Southern Baptist Historical Library and Archives, Nashville, TN, 21–22; Flynt and Berkley, *Taking Christianity to China*, 152; *Southern Baptist Missionary Journal* (1847): 9 and (1849): 44.

[7] *Annual of the SBC* (1849): 49, 51, and (1855): 73–89 passim

Lottie Moon. In forcefulness of personality, both Martha and her husband stand out in the history of Baptists trying to convert the Chinese to Christianity. Because of this, a considerable portion of their story before going to China and during their service there is appropriate for this study. Martha Foster, from Tuscaloosa County, Alabama, was the daughter of a substantial planter. She was converted in a revival meeting at the LaFayette Baptist Church in 1845. Being a thoroughgoing romantic, Martha fell in love several times, moving on from one failed romance to another. She admitted to being fickle, but she had a variety of interests and was given to introspection. She liked to write, study religion, and observe politics. As a young teacher she came to believe that she was called to be a missionary in China. T. P. Crawford was a Kentuckian, and he too came to feel that he was called to go to China. Upon going to Richmond to apply at the FMB he was told that he needed a wife in order to make a successful application. He was told of Martha Foster and her interest in China, and he struck out for Alabama to meet her. They met in Clinton, Alabama on 16 February 1851. Crawford proposed that they marry and go to China together. For ten days they thought the matter over, finally deciding that it was a bad idea because they did not love each other. Crawford left, but returned, by which time both had changed their minds. Thus, they began a "mutual attachment" that was to be "developed in the future." On 12 March 1851, at age twenty-one, Martha was married to T. P. Crawford by Dr. Basil Manly, Baptist preacher and president of the University of Alabama.[8]

On 17 November 1851 the newly married Crawfords sailed for China, fully realizing that a "marriage of convenience" had become their vehicle for their "commitment to China missions." Because of conflicting personalities, the Crawfords were not always at peace in their marriage or in their ideas regarding the

---

[8] Flynt and Berkley, *Taking Christianity to China*, 35, 48–49, 50–51.

mission enterprise in China. Whether they grew to love one another truly is hard to judge. They did not seem to expect much from their marriage in that regard, but before her husband died, Martha claimed that they had "more than the ordinary share of wedded happiness."[9]

Among the other missionaries whom the Crawfords met in Shanghai and with whom they were to work were I. J. and Virginia Roberts. Martha concluded that Mrs. Roberts was a mental case, for she refused to be left alone with Chinese people. Virginia constantly clung to Martha, becoming agitated when the latter left her by herself in a room. Loathing the sight of the Chinese, as Virginia did, she was a most unhappy person. She even threatened to commit suicide. On one occasion the Crawfords found her beating her head against a wall. The Robertses quarreled often, and Virginia made it clear that if she ever returned home, she would not come back to China, whether or not her husband did. Martha came to regard Roberts as a cruel man and blamed him for Virginia's "advanced case of insanity." The question remains: which of the Robertses was more insane? In 1855 Virginia took her two children back to the United States, while I. J., who had become swept up in the Taiping Rebellion, went to live for a year among the Taiping rebels. Though claiming to be Christians, the Taiping rebels adhered to a bizarre brand of Christianity. After the rebels were finally defeated by the Ching dynasty they had hoped to replace, Roberts returned to the United States and lived with a niece in Illinois until he died of leprosy.[10]

After eleven years in Shanghai the Crawfords left there in 1863 for health reasons and went to a new work just beginning in Shantung Province to the north. As she had in Shanghai, Martha opened a school at Tengchow. She wrote accounts of her work

---

[9] Ibid., 51–52.
[10] Ibid., 216–17.

and sent them home, where they were published in the *Alabama Baptist.* She corresponded with the Moon sisters, who contributed $45 in gold to her school. Martha urged Eddie Moon to apply to the FMB for an appointment to be a missionary, offering her a place to live in the Crawford home. Eddie did apply, was appointed, and lived with the Crawfords in Tengchow before persuading her soon-to-be famous sister to join her there.[11]

Both Martha and T. P. Crawford set out to learn Chinese, and both came close to mastering the language. However, because Martha progressed faster and was said to speak the language like a native, Crawford was jealous of his wife. Over the coming years Martha dedicated herself to the work of teaching children and trying to win Chinese women to Christ, both by inviting them to her home and using it as a chapel and by witnessing to them in their own homes. A bright, energetic woman, Martha wrote six books in English, including a novel and books on Christian doctrine. Although Martha made it a point not to teach men, there were times when she went into the countryside with only fellow women missionaries, and since there was no male missionary present, she allowed men to stay in the background and listen. One can only wonder how the FMB and the SBC might have reacted to news that Martha had indirectly taught Chinese males, since accounts on the work of the Crawfords in the FMB reports to the denomination pointedly declared that she was working with children, teaching them "arithmetic, geography, grammar, vocal music, Scripture history, New Testament Evidences of Christianity and other religious books." Other than that, Mrs. Crawford, the reports said, was visiting home to home to convert and teach "those of her own sex."[12]

---

[11] Ibid., 14, 199.

[12] *Annual of the SBC* (1870): 10, 12; Flynt and Berkley, *Taking Christianity to China*, 63–64, 131, 152; Amanda Porterfield, *Feminine Spirituality in America* (Philadelphia: Temple University Press, 1980) 170–71.

Obviously the FMB report was not totally accurate in its statements regarding Martha Crawford's activities.

Even so, Martha would have agreed with the spirit of the report. She eventually came to believe that women missionaries should become preachers, but that they should limit their public addresses to audiences of their own sex only. Although she was a strong-willed woman who was determined to accomplish the work to which she believed God had called her, Martha remained a product of the Southern Baptist culture that had molded her. In 1848 she had been scornful of the Seneca Falls Convention, attacking the sentiments that were proclaimed by those who attended. In spite of the fact that—after adjusting to the realities of the situation in China—she allowed men to listen while she taught women during her inland tours (if no male missionary was along), she remained committed to the conventional belief in the "two spheres." This, of course, required women not to engage in work that was reserved for men. In a long letter to the *Alabama Baptist* in 1891 Martha stated that a woman who felt the call to be a missionary should not "forget her sex and perform the labors appropriate only to men." She noted that Southern Baptist women missionaries in China maintained "the same modest, ladylike deportment" they maintained in the homeland. They taught women and children and did not preach. When approached by inquiring male Chinese, women missionaries told them that conversation between the sexes was improper.[13] One is forced to conclude that Martha was not one hundred percent honest in her statements to Alabama Baptists, knowing that she must keep up certain appearances. After all, Southern Baptists and Southern culture demanded that women refrain from instructing men, whether in Alabama or in China.

---

[13] *Alabama Baptist* (27 August 1891) 2–3; Flynt and Berkley, *Taking Christianity to China*, 132, 152–53, 199, 208–209.

Martha accomplished much, perhaps in spite of her husband, who sooner or later seemed to clash with everyone around him. Among the numerous women with whom she worked was Mrs. J. B. Hartwell, operator of a small school at Tengchow. The J. B. Hartwells and the T. P. Crawfords had lived together for a time in Shanghai, but in an atmosphere of tension. Yet, after the Hartwells went to Tengchow to pioneer missionary work there, the Crawfords followed. However, the friction between T. P Crawford and J. B. Hartwell convinced them that they should live in different houses and go to different churches. Crawford founded a church that floundered, while Hartwell's church grew and prospered. The two men never got along, and Martha seems to have had little to do with Eliza Hartwell, who died on 9 June 1870 after nearly ten years of dedication to her work in China. Mrs. Hartwell was eulogized in the FMB's report to the 1871 convention in touching words that read, "For the last year she has suffered with failing health, and, by advice of the physician, she was preparing for a season to return to her native land; but her Divine Master had determined she should fall in the field of her labor, and should find a grave among those for whose salvation she had patiently toiled and suffered."[14] Perhaps the eulogy was merely a matter of protocol, but the FMB apparently thought highly of Mrs. Hartwell's work in China, regardless of what the Crawfords thought of the Hartwells.

A more amiable relationship existed between the Crawfords and Mrs. J. Landrum Holmes who left the United States in 1870 to join them in Shantung Province. In 1871 T. P. Crawford reported that "sister Holmes" had "just moved to her new and convenient house" and had opened her girls' school with four pupils and the prospect of others soon. Working closely with Martha, Mrs. Holmes seemed "very happy and hopeful."

---

[14] *Annual of the SBC* (1871): 41–42; Flynt and Berkley, *Taking Christianity to China*, 60, 263–64.

Southern Baptist work was definitely growing in China, and women were a big part of it. They were in Canton, Shanghai, and Shantung Province. Martha Crawford seemed to work well with most of the women, while her husband seemed to work well with no one, not even his wife. While he apparently liked Eddie Moon and helped bring Lottie to China, he eventually fell out with the latter. Martha and Lottie, on the other hand, worked together harmoniously. Crawford and his wife began to drift apart, and in 1878 he abruptly left. He returned the next year, but the marital differences were not resolved. In 1881 Martha left for Alabama, separating from her husband for almost two years. When she returned in 1883, she consented to "be a good wife" and abide by T. P.'s wishes. To please him she closed down her school, which caused Lottie Moon to become alienated from T. P., but not from Martha. They continued to work together. Martha not only closed her school; she also agreed to follow her husband's plan to make all missions self-supporting, a plan that soon created friction between the various missionaries in China and between Crawford and the FMB.[15]

T. P. Crawford had formulated a philosophy of missions known as "Gospel Missionism." He wanted to eliminate all schools operated by the China mission (This was his reason for insisting that Martha close her school.), championing "immediate self-support as the only biblical method in missionary work." The idea that all missions ought to be self-supporting from the outset became an obsession with Crawford and put him squarely at odds with the FMB. When the FMB opposed his plan, Crawford, his wife, and several other missionaries who supported "Gospel Missionism" resigned from the FMB. Eventually Crawford and his wife left Tengchow and settled in Taian in western Shantung, the center of the handful of missionaries who were part of T. P.'s Gospel Mission. In 1901

---

[15] Flynt and Berkley, *Taking Christianity to China*, 218–19.

the Crawfords returned to the United States. A year later T. P. died, and Martha, at age seventy-two, returned to Taian and stayed until her death seven years later. During those seven years she lived before a sacred mountain, telling pilgrims who passed by about Christ. Two years before her death she persuaded the Gospel Mission group to return to the FMB. When she died at age seventy-nine in 1909, she was buried, at her request, in Tengchow.[16] Thus a Southern Baptist woman, who had striven mightily to obey both God and the Southern culture that had shaped her, passed from this earth in a foreign land she adopted and loved so much that she gave over fifty years of her life in service there. Her life and, especially, her missionary career in China demonstrate that it was often difficult to reconcile the demands of both God and culture.

The Crawfords at one juncture concluded that their life's work was a failure and blamed the FMB for it. This was surely an unwarranted conclusion, for however one assesses the results of their efforts as missionaries, no one could argue that the Crawfords were failures, unless they concluded that the entire Christian missionary effort in China was a failure. After all, only a small percentage of Chinese were ever converted to the Christian faith by all the missionaries who ever went to China. While it is true that the Crawfords were responsible for the conversion and baptism of only a few hundred Chinese during their fifty years in China, their percentage of converts was probably not that insignificant when compared to others. They certainly injected some life and enthusiasm into Southern Baptist work in China, even though T. P. proposed the controversial Gospel Mission plan. Besides, the Crawfords' work could be judged a success on the basis that it was they who were most instrumental in getting Lottie Moon to China. No single

---

[16] Allen, *The New Lottie Moon Story*, 250–51; Estep, *Whole Gospel, Whole World*, 139–42, 144, 173–74; Flynt and Berkley, *Taking Christianity to China*, 136, 220; Porterfield, *Feminine Spirituality in America*, 171.

missionary did as much toward establishing Southern Baptist mission work in China or in general as did Lottie Moon. In the process she opened the door so that Southern Baptist women could gain some recognition and status, even though the status gained fell short of total equality with Southern Baptist men. Because of her monumental contribution to Southern Baptist missions, Moon deserves a great deal of space in this study.

Charlotte Diggs ("Lottie") Moon was born 12 December 1840 to a privileged family in Albemarle County, Virginia. She attended the best schools, studying at Hollins College and receiving a master's degree from Albemarle Female Institute in 1861. She was one of the first women in the South to earn a master's degree. At age sixteen, while a student at Albemarle, she was converted under the preaching of the eminent Baptist minister John A. Broadus at the First Baptist Church of Charlottesville. Until then Lottie had been regarded as a skeptic by friends and fellow students. She graduated in 1861 with the reputation of being the most scholarly student at Albemarle. She excelled at languages—Greek, Latin, and French. She was proficient in Italian and Spanish as well. She studied Hebrew in independent study, apparently under the direction of Crawford H. Toy, whose name would shortly be known throughout Southern Baptist circles. John Broadus called Lottie Moon the most educated woman in the South.[17]

About two years after Lottie was converted, her older sister Orianna ("Orie") was converted and became a Disciples of Christ communicant, but prior to that she was swept up in the Women's Rights movement that followed the Seneca Falls Convention. She entered medical school and became one of the first women in America to earn a medical degree. Since women did not make a

---

[17] Catherine B. Allen, *Laborers Together with God: 22 Great Women in Baptist Life* (Birmingham AL: Woman's Missionary Union, 1987) 236–37; Allen, *The New Lottie Moon Story*, 34–35, 38–39; Estep, *Whole Gospel, Whole World*, 144–46; McBeth, *Women in Baptist Life*, 90–91.

living practicing medicine in the South, she served for a time as a medical missionary to Jerusalem for her church. Lottie, for several years, chose a teaching career, going in 1866 to Danville, Kentucky, where she was a popular teacher at Danville Female Academy. She attended and taught Sunday school at Danville's First Baptist Church. In Danville she first began to think of China, but she soon had to face the illness and death of her mother, Anna Marie Moon. That occurred on 21 June 1870, with Lottie standing and weeping beside her mother's bed. Lottie's father had died earlier aboard a steamboat during an outbreak of fire.[18]

After the death of her parents Lottie apparently turned down several young men who pursued her hand in marriage and moved to Cartersville, Georgia, with her close friend Anna Cunningham Safford, the daughter of a Presbyterian missionary. Moon and Safford taught school together in Cartersville and remained lifelong friends. The two women conducted a fashionable girls school until Lottie heard her call to foreign missions "as clear as a bell." At some point in her short teaching career Lottie had expressed herself on the "woman question" in the pages of the *Religious Herald.* She called for making greater use of women in promoting the Christian cause and even advocated having two deaconesses in all Baptist churches. Some Southern Baptist men, particularly Henry A. Tupper, had begun to sympathize with such views, and the FMB appointed Lottie to China (as it had her sister the year before) on 7 July 1873. She was assigned to Tengchow, where she would join the Crawfords and her sister Eddie.[19]

For a tiny woman of perhaps four and a half feet in height, Lottie Moon proved to be a durable physical specimen

---

[18] Allen, *The New Lottie Moon Story*, 23, 30–31, 53–56; Estep, *Whole Gospel, Whole World*, 144–146; McBeth, *Women in Baptist Life*, 90–91.

[19] Allen, *The New Lottie Moon Story*, 60–62; Estep, *Whole Gospel, Whole World*, 144–146; McBeth, *Women in Baptist Life*, 90–91.

throughout most of her forty years in China. The beginning of her stint was somewhat rough, as she was seasick for twenty-five days on her voyage across the Pacific. Her first step on Far Eastern soil was in Japan before she sailed on to China. The petite Miss Moon had blue eyes and dark brown hair. She was not pretty, but she had a forceful personality. She was strong-willed and, to a point, she championed women's rights. By no means a flaming radical and perhaps not even as forward as her sister Orie, Lottie was not one to let men run over her—not even T. P. Crawford. Within a year of her arrival in Tengchow, Lottie bemoaned the lack of Baptist workers, claiming that Southern Baptists were being put to shame by Presbyterians. She began by opening a girls' school, while her sister Eddie had a day school for boys, which had an enrollment of thirteen pupils in 1874. Eddie was more delicate than Lottie, and in 1876 she was overcome by culture shock and fell ill. The fact that the Chinese she encountered often attacked her verbally, calling her "devil woman," no doubt contributed significantly to Eddie's declining health and interest in remaining a missionary. Lottie insisted that her sister return to Virginia. In 1877 Eddie, accompanied by Lottie, went home to Viewmont in Albemarle County.[20]

Lottie did not tarry long in Virginia. On 8 November 1877 she sailed again for China aboard the *Tokio Maru*. Upon her return to Tengchow she expected "to establish a school for children of the higher class of people." Money to help build her house in which she would operate the school was to be raised "by the ladies of Virginia and Georgia." She had already had her seasoning in the house of the contentious T. P. Crawford before taking Eddie home to Virginia. She had immediately undertaken to learn Mandarin and had then moved on to the other dialects of the region, eventually mastering all of them. She had also been

---

[20] Allen, *Laborers Together with God*, 237–39; Allen, *The New Lottie Moon Story*, 11, 79–80, 108–11, 119; *Annual of the SBC* (1874): 33–34 and (1877): 39, 43; Flynt and Berkley, *Taking Christianity to China*, 199.

introduced to the infighting between Crawford and J. B. Hartwell. Even though Hartwell's North Street Church was growing and Crawford's Monument Street Church was not, the FMB declared that Crawford's church should merge with Hartwell's under Crawford's direction. A majority of the missionaries in the area sided with Crawford and endorsed his evolving views that would ultimately cause him and his Gospel Mission followers to break with the FMB. Rather than serve under the direction of Crawford at Tengchow, Hartwell apparently left the mission for a while, and Lottie Moon lived for a long time at his North Street compound. Eventually she moved into a house at the "Little Cross Roads." It became her permanent home. In the end Hartwell returned to Tengchow with a new team of missionaries, and Crawford went into the interior to Taian. Even though Lottie Moon quarreled with Crawford, she seems to have adopted some of his views, and on more than one occasion, she was critical of the FMB. Ultimately, she split with Crawford, accusing the Gospel Mission group of setting up their own board. Still, she and Martha remained close friends and continued to work together at times.[21]

In 1878 Lottie reopened the school that was "formerly under her sister's care" and had thirteen girl students. She attempted but failed to buy some property to build a house on North Street. Working with her at this point was Sallie (Mrs. J. Landrum) Holmes. Both women were concerned about Chinese girls having their feet bound, and they tried, unsuccessfully for the most part, to persuade the mothers of their students to unbind them. Despite their quarrels with some Chinese customs, the school established by Moon and Holmes continued to grow, having an enrollment of thirty-seven by 1884. The FMB always

---

[21] Allen, *The New Lottie Moon Story*, 87–93, 105–107, 119, 123; *Annual of the SBC* (1873): 43; (1878): 47; and (1879): 58; Leon McBeth, *Women in Baptist Life* (Nashville: Broadman Press, 1979) 91; Flynt and Berkley, *Taking Christianity to China*, 220, 268.

reported Lottie's work as among "women and girls" so that the SBC would know she was not speaking to men. By the mid-1880s there was a number of women working in China, including several single women, but they went to other missions, not to Tengchow. At one point after Sallie Holmes left, Lottie was briefly the only Southern Baptist missionary in North China. About the time she decided to give up her school and go into the countryside to conduct "city visiting"—in 1883 or 1884—she considered marrying her old professor, Crawford H. Toy. The controversial Toy, because of his liberal views, had been forced out of his position at Southern Baptist Theological Seminary and had become a professor at Harvard University. Lottie alerted her family to be prepared for a wedding, but in the end the wedding plans fell through. No one knows why, though it has been alleged that Lottie dropped the wedding plans because of Toy's heterodox religious views. It has also been asserted that Lottie simply could not give up her work in China.[22]

The mid-1880s must have been hard years for Lottie Moon. Quarreling with T. P. Crawford, agonizing over whether to leave China for the easier life of a Harvard professor's wife, and giving up her school to evangelize the countryside must have troubled her. It could not have been easy to stay friends with Martha Crawford while carrying on verbal battles with T. P., especially after 1885 when she flatly rejected Crawford's view that Chinese converts should carry on their own mission work without help from the FMB. Not only did she reject it, she recommended that the FMB reject it, too, which it did. Moon must have known that she would always be single if she spurned Crawford Toy's marriage proposal. The decision she made was to do the work she believed God had called her to do, and that was to present Christ to the Chinese. To do it most effectively, she was willing to do

---

[22] Allen, *Laborers Together with God*, 238–39; Allen, *The New Lottie Moon Story*, 124–26, 139, 144, 147; *Annual of the SBC* (1879): 58; (1883): appendix A; and (1884): appendix B.

what other women had never dared to do before. She opened an interior mission all by herself at Pingtu, a heavily populated city. Upon her arrival, she was the only foreigner in the city. At her new mission she lived like the Chinese and won the friendship of her neighbors. A major benefit of being there was that she was free from contact with T. P. Crawford and his dictatorial ways. She was successful, winning some converts as she taught out in the open and on threshing floors. Eventually, though, she returned to Tengchow and reopened her school.[23]

Whether teaching children at Pingtu or Tengchow or traveling across the countryside of Shantung Province with Sallie Holmes or Martha Crawford, Lottie Moon showed the utmost respect for the Chinese by dressing like them and living like them. Even though she was occasionally called a "foreign devil" and was threatened with death, she persisted in her work. She was not broken in spirit, as many missionaries were, by some ghastly sights that were seen along Chinese roads—dogs devouring human corpses and babies left alone to die. Everywhere there was inadequate housing, spoiled food, and wretched medical care. In spite of it all, Lottie Moon still regarded China as the world's most civilized nation. From sun up to sun down she worked tirelessly, day in and day out, teaching in her home or someone else's. She did her best to follow the conventions of the time—the conventions so sacrosanct in the American South and in China—by keeping her place as a woman and not speaking when men were present. Eventually, though, she had to disregard convention, for some Chinese men wanted to hear what she had to say, and she found herself speaking to mixed crowds of men, women, and children in the countryside. She could not resist, she said, because there were "so many souls before me sunk in heathen darkness." Still, she was careful to avoid giving the

---

[23] Allen, *Laborers Together with God*, 238–39; Allen, *The New Lottie Moon Story*, 147, 149–51, 155; Estep, *Whole Gospel, Whole World*, 147–49.

impression that she "preached" to men. When speaking in the open air, she could not prevent men from wandering into the crowd of women and children to whom she was speaking, but indoors she taught women and children in one room while allowing men to sit in another and eavesdrop. When Chinese men asked her to preach to them, she replied that "it was not the custom of the ancient church that women preach to men." Even so, all the pretensions of not preaching to men and all the Southern Baptist denials of women missionaries preaching to men notwithstanding, Lottie Moon, and other missionary women such as Martha Crawford and Willie Kelly, preached to Chinese men. In fact, one of Lottie Moon's converts was a man named Li Show-ting, who became the greatest Christian evangelist in North China, baptizing over ten thousand converts.[24]

During the mid-1880s, when Lottie Moon and Martha Crawford were transforming the role of women missionaries in China, Moon quarreled not only with T. P. Crawford, but the FMB as well. She upset tradition by demanding that single women, if not married ones, should participate in meetings to plan Chinese mission work. She wrote, "Simple justice demands that women should have equal rights with men in mission meetings and in the conduct of their work." When the FMB quoted her position and followed it with a disclaimer, Lottie threatened twice in 1885 to resign. In her eyes, she was the equal of men in handling mission affairs, and she refused to be treated as a subordinate. Apparently, in the face of Lottie's threats to quit if she were not given a vote at the yearly mission meetings, the FMB yielded, although other women did as they were expected and remained silent at the meetings. Some male

---

[24] Allen, *The New Lottie Moon Story*, 96, 98–99, 103, 108–109, 127–28, 130, 162–68, 178–80, 184; Flynt and Berkley, *Taking Christianity to China*, 87, 232, 234.

missionaries were offended by her refusal to accept the traditional silent role of the woman missionary.[25]

In 1887 the state WMU central committees were on the verge of establishing a national organization, the purpose of which was to increase support to Southern Baptist missionaries. Many Southern Baptist men objected to such an organization for a variety of reasons, one being that a national WMU would usurp the authority of men in the mission enterprise. Lottie Moon was sensitive to such charges, and had much to say on the subject. She contended that "we do not need to adopt plans or methods unsuitable to the views, or repugnant to the tastes of our brethren. What we want is not power, but simply combination [union] in order to elicit the largest possible giving." She recommended organizing in subordination to the FMB. Instead of doing that, however, the WMU established itself the following year in Richmond as independent of but auxiliary to the SBC, but with every intention of cooperating as much as possible with the FMB. It was about this same time that Lottie suggested a week of prayer for foreign missions and a special offering for foreign missions at Christmastime. That offering was soon institutionalized, and, thirty-one years after she recommended it (1918), it was named the Lottie Moon Christmas Offering upon the recommendation of Annie Armstrong.[26]

During the controversy over the organization of a national WMU and the flap over Moon's demands that she have a voice in planning the mission work in China, she decided that missionaries should have a furlough after serving ten consecutive

---

[25] Allen, *The New Lottie Moon Story*, 42; Janet W. James, ed., *Women in American Religion* (Philadelphia: University of Pennsylvania Press, 1976) 121–22; McBeth, *Women in Baptist Life*, 91.

[26] Allen, *Laborers Together with God*, 240–41; Allen, *The New Lottie Moon Story*, 169–70; Hunt, *History of Woman's Missionary Union*, 24; Leon McBeth, "The Role of Women in Southern Baptist History," *Baptist History & Heritage* (January 1977): 6.

years in the field. In 1887 she pointed out that she had not been home in ten years and asked H. A. Tupper for a furlough, while at the same time pleading continuously for more missionaries to be sent to help her and Martha Crawford. Reluctantly, the FMB agreed to her request, but she resolved not to leave China until June 1888. At this juncture she seems to have made an uneasy peace with T. P. Crawford in the interest of the greater good. She even signed his "Articles of Agreement" before leaving on her furlough. Originally planning to sail for home in 1888, Lottie was delayed, not getting away from her work until 1890. After fourteen straight years in China, at long last she sailed for America on the *Empress of China*. Once in Virginia she discussed with H. A. Tupper the "Articles of Agreement" that Crawford was persuading various missionaries in China to sign. The articles spelled out the broad principles of self-support upon which Crawford's Gospel Missionism was based. Tupper wanted to know from Moon who the signers were and which of them were friends of the FMB. The secretary feared that Lottie Moon was the only one, and he worried about the damage that Crawford might do in her absence.[27]

Lottie Moon's furlough lasted over two years. In 1892, now "fat and fiftyish" according to her biographer, she took the opportunity to attend the annual WMU meeting and the meeting of the SBC in Atlanta. Already a legend among Southern Baptist women who took an interest in missions, Lottie was the center of attention at the WMU meeting. Praised for her nineteen years of service in China, she stood in her Chinese robes to be recognized. There is no evidence of any attention being called to her presence at the SBC meeting.[28] One can only presume that she was at least recognized and thanked for her years of service in China, but that is strictly a presumption.

---

[27] Allen, *The New Lottie Moon Story*, 132, 134, 164–71, 186–89, 195.
[28] Ibid., 199.

On 21 November 1893 Lottie Moon boarded the *China* and sailed back to her mission field. Once there, she broke with T. P. Crawford once and for all, accusing the Gospel Mission crowd of having set up their own mission board. Lottie learned that during the previous year T. P. had pressured Martha Crawford to resign from the FMB, three years after he and some of his followers had resigned. The Crawfordites had withdrawn into the interior, far from Pingtu and Tengchow, and Lottie was glad to be rid of them. Meanwhile, the Gospel Mission crowd spread the word that the FMB was overpaying the missionaries it sent to China, prompting R. J. Willingham, Tupper's succesor as FMB secretary, to ask missionaries sponsored by the board to take a salary cut.[29]

During the 1890s Moon apparently came to believe that she had earned the right to bend convention a bit. She taught Bible classes with men present. China soon experienced turbulent times because of a war with Japan, during which Moon was accused of being a Japanese spy. Then came the famous Boxer Rebellion in 1900. The Boxers were determined to drive all foreigners from their land. To them there was no such thing as a well-meaning foreigner, not even the venerable lady missionary from Pingtu and Tengchow. During a trip to Pingtu in 1900, she found it necessary to disguise herself as a male Chinese official in order to avoid harassment or worse at the hands of the xenophobic Boxers. The disguise worked, but eventually Chinese Christians found it necessary to disassociate themselves from foreign missionaries to avoid being killed. Ultimately all foreigners were ordered out of Shantung Province by the consul at Tengchow. Lottie Moon fled first to Chefoo, then Shanghai, and finally to Japan, where, for less than a year, she served as a missionary.[30]

---

[29] Ibid.,196–97, 199, 202, 204, 206.
[30] Ibid., 209, 217–20, 223–24; Flynt and Berkley, *Taking Christianity to China*, 269, 286, 297–98.

With the passing of years Lottie began to lose her physical vitality. She became frail. So many years of teaching and evangelizing took a toll on her throat, and her voice weakened. Yet, she still had a fighting spirit and clashed with J. B. Hartwell in 1901 on the role of single female missionaries. She thought unmarried women missionaries should work in the country and not the city, arguing that married women could handle the work there. Apparently the Hartwells became jealous of her because of the high esteem in which she was held in North China and by the FMB. Through her work and letters to people back home, many of which found their way into Baptist journals, she inspired many Southern Baptist women to become involved in the cause of missions.[31]

In 1902 Lottie began preparing for what would be her last furlough to America. She had American clothes made for herself, though she had not worn anything but Chinese clothing in nine years. This was her third trip home since first going to China in 1873. She had gained weight and lost teeth, and both contributed to her declining health. Back home for a year, she spoke many times, but to women only. On occasion men slipped into the back of the room, as did FMB Secretary R. J. Willingham. Lottie pretended not to see them. At one point during her visit she raised a provocative question: Why should Southern Baptists send missionaries to Africa when white people, including Southern Baptists, would not go and minister to poor blacks in the United States? Her visit ended on 15 February 1904 when she told her relatives goodbye for what she believed would be the last time. Arriving back in China, she returned to her home at the Little Cross Roads and committed herself as never before to academic education. The winds of revolution were rising in China, and the country became "education hungry." This dedicated teacher of

---

[31] Allen, *The New Lottie Moon Story*, 217–19, 229, 247; McBeth, *Women in Southern Baptist Life*, 92.

Christianity to the Chinese rose to *grande dame* status all over
North China.[32]

Lottie Moon's final years in China were troubling ones. She
had to confront several problems in 1904, including the threat of
another Boxer uprising. Remembering the terror associated with
the Boxer Rebellion of 1900, she went out of her way to avoid
the wrath of these rabid nationalist Chinese who looked with
favor on no foreigner. Even though T. P. Crawford had died in
the United States in 1902, advocates of the Gospel Mission
movement were still around, and they had little use for Lottie
Moon. Apparently seeking revenge for her opposition to them,
they sent word to people in Georgia that she was not teaching
according "to fundamental Southern Baptist tenets." The
vindictive Gospel Missionists mentioned the "Toy influence,"
which Southern Baptists regarded as heresy. Two women claimed
that Martha Crawford had made the accusation, but Martha
expressed her confidence in her longtime cohort. R. J.
Willingham said that during her thirty years of service, no one
had ever accused Lottie of heresy before. She herself said, "I
have never taught contrary to the usual views of the Southern
Baptists. I am trying...to lead the Chinese to the Lord Jesus."
The discussion concerning Moon's theology soon ceased.[33]

In spite of political turmoil and hostile criticism from the
Gospel Mission crowd, Lottie persisted in her work. Because
China was modernizing, there was a demand for the Chinese to
learn English. She taught it in her school to all who came—even
men. During times of famine in China she starved herself to give
food to the Chinese, and when the FMB came upon hard times
she forfeited her salary and even lent the board money. When
revolution erupted in China in 1911, it became dangerous to
travel. Lottie traveled anyway. She was overjoyed in 1912 when

---

[32] Allen, *The New Lottie Moon Story*, 230, 237–40, 242, 245, 247.
[33] Ibid., 245–246, 250.

China became a republic and began using the Christian calendar. Religious liberty was proclaimed, and Moon praised Sun Yat-sen, China's new leader. By this time she was something of a pathetic figure, carrying only fifty pounds on her short frame. Her health gone, Lottie became depressed and *imagined* that she was the worst of sinners and that she was standing on the brink of financial ruin. Her depression no doubt stemmed in part from news that her beloved sister, Eddie, had committed suicide in 1908. She wrote, "I pray that no missionary will ever be as lonely as I have been." [34]

For a long time the FMB had urged Lottie to come home, but she had resisted. At last there was no choice. She was not eating and was dangerously underweight. Her fellow missionaries and the FMB insisted that she go home to recover. The FMB sent registered nurse Cynthia Miller to escort the famous missionary home. On the way, Lottie Moon died, while the ship on which she sailed, the *Manchuria*, was taking on coal at the port of Kobe, Japan. Her death occurred on 24 December 1912. Cynthia Miller reported that she died of "meloncholia and senility." Two days after her death, Lottie Moon was cremated in Yokohama. Her ashes were delivered eventually to her home at Crewe, Virginia, where they were buried beside her brother Isaac.[35]

Lottie Moon and her work had been mentioned often through the years in the *Annual of the Southern Baptist Convention*, but she had never been highly praised. Finally, in the 1913 *Annual,* she was called "a queenly saint among missionaries" who had "passed to her reward on the 24th of December, 1912." It was added, "For forty years she worked

---

[34] Allen, *The New Lottie Moon Story*, 258, 272–73, 275–76, 289–90; Estep, *Whole Gospel, Whole World*, 149–50.

[35] Allen, *Laborers Together with God*, 241; Allen, *The New Lottie Moon Story*, 276–77, 286–90; Estep, *Whole Gospel, Whole World*, 149–50; McBeth, *Women in Baptist Life*, 92.

nobly."[36] Thus, the most famous missionary ever sent out by
Southern Baptists passed into the pages of history. Many
Southern Baptist women, both before and after her death,
idolized her, as did the more enlightened Southern Baptist men.
Even though she was a woman of her own time, urging women to
abide by their traditional roles and advising WMU leaders to defer
to the male leaders of the Foreign Mission Board and the Home
Mission Board, she insisted on being treated equally in the
planning of mission work in North China. Moreover, because she
believed that the SBC did not send enough missionaries to China
to do the work of missions adequately, she even taught men and
led them to Christ on the sly. She would not allow herself to be
pushed around by either T. P. Crawford or the FMB, ultimately
distancing herself from Crawford (T. P. but not Martha) and
threatening to quit if the FMB did not allow her a voice and a
vote in the missionary planning meetings. While she certainly
did not eliminate male chauvinism in the SBC or at the FMB, she
still advanced the cause of women by giving single women
missionaries an honored place in the foreign mission enterprise.
Because of her, the single women who served at the same time
she did and after she did were accorded greater respect.

Even before Lottie Moon's death there were other women
in China and on other mission fields who were making significant
contributions, and they would continue along the noble path that
she had pioneered. Lula Whilden of Alabama actually preceded
Moon in China by a year, and others arrived both before and
after Lottie's death. Notable among them were Mary Anderson,
Addie Cox, Janie Lowrey Graves, Alice Huey, Willie Kelly, and
Cynthia Miller. Anderson, who was the niece of Janie Lowrey
Graves, spent eighteen years in China (1917–1935), teaching at
Pei Tao Academy for girls in Canton. She resented the treatment
of single female missionaries by the FMB, which referred to them

---

[36] *Annual of the SBC* (1913): 102–103.

as "female missionary assistants." She had apparently imbibed some of the views of the Gospel Mission group, favoring Chinese control of her school. This put her at loggerheads with the FMB and prompted her to resign and return to Alabama in 1935.[37]

Most of these women, as well as some others, eventually abandoned the notion that women must refrain from preaching and stick strictly to teaching women and children. Cynthia Miller, a nurse by profession, ultimately gave up nursing and teaching to spend all of her time doing evangelism. She traveled with Peyton Stephens and his wife and helped them conduct American-style tent revivals. Stephens, often referred to as "China's Billy Sunday," spoke to men in the tent, while Miller and her "Bible woman" went from house to house to witness to Chinese women. Miller served in China for thirty-one years.[38]

No single female missionary, other than Lottie Moon, was more assertive than Willie Hayes Kelly. Born in Wilcox County, Alabama, Kelly went to China in 1893. Her salary was paid by the Alabama WMU because the FMB could not afford to pay her. She engaged in teaching and evangelism, devoting most of her time to women's work after 1904. She held summer Bible schools for children in Shanghai. During the 1930s she and Addie Cox were involved in "refugee ministries," meaning that they helped Chinese who were displaced by Japanese offensives in China. They preached to the refugees and provided them with food and other assistance. She not only preached in China, she had herself and two Chinese women made deacons at the North Gate Baptist Church in Shanghai. In 1937 she was forced to leave for home because of the full-scale invasion of China by the Japanese. During her forty-four years as a missionary Willie went home on furlough occasionally, and while in the United States, she spoke at many state meetings. Her fame as a missionary prompted SBC

---

[37] Flynt and Berkley, *Taking Christianity to China*, 22, 161, 163, 174, 189, 199–200.

[38] Ibid., 40–41, 155, 189, 211.

officials to invite her to speak at the 1938 annual convention. Among women missionaries to China, only Lottie Moon's name looms larger than Willie Kelly's.[39]

For many years far more women went to China than to any other country. By 1913 sixty-seven women had gone to China as missionaries, while only twenty-five had gone to Africa; thirty to Mexico; nineteen to Brazil; and only six, four, and one to Japan, Italy, and Argentina respectively. On the field in 1913 were ninety-three in China, five in Africa, three in Italy, twenty-two in Brazil, sixteen in Mexico, eight in Argentina, and nine in Japan. One of the early missionaries to Africa was Mrs. W. J. David, who accompanied her husband in 1879 to serve in Abeokuta, Nigeria. Many other women went out under the auspices of the FMB, some single and others to accompany their husbands. Between 1848 and 1992 over forty women died while in service on various missions fields. A large number of women served as missionaries longer than thirty years and some for forty or more. Except for Martha Crawford, only one served for more than fifty years—Mrs. William Buck (Anne) Bagby, who served in Brazil.[40]

Meanwhile, a few women had become home missionaries under the sponsorship of the Home Mission Board, but the HMB appointed far fewer women than did the FMB. By 1883 Mrs. J. L. Sanford and Mrs. J. B. Hartwell served in San Francisco, probably in the Chinese community primarily. Mrs. H. F. Buckner and several other women went as missionaries to the Creek Nation, but Mrs. Buckner's appointment came after the

---

[39] Wayne Flynt, *Alabama Baptists: Southern Baptists in the Heart of Dixie* (Tuscaloosa and London: The University of Alabama Press, 1998) 240–41; Flynt and Berkley, *Taking Christianity to China*, 21, 138, 144, 155, 161, 165.

[40] *Annual of the SBC* (1880): 39, 41; Estep, *Whole Gospel, Whole World*, 397–418 passim; Flynt and Berkley, *Taking Christianity to China*, 13; Fannie E. S. Heck, *In Royal Service: The Mission Work of Southern Baptist Women* (Richmond: Foreign Mission Board, 1913) 226–97 passim, 362–64, 366–69.

death of her husband. A century later in 1983 the number of single women missionaries sent out by the FMB was about 7.8 percent of the total number of missionaries, while the HMB appointed 3,500 missionaries in 1984, and only 174 women were designated as the primary worker. Overall, the women sent out by the two mission boards—particularly the single women—did not make up large numbers, but in quality of service they proved to be some of the greatest missionaries who carried the SBC banner to the mission fields both at home and abroad.[41]

While the SBC does not have a tradition of mistreating its women missionaries, generally speaking, women have never been treated by either of its mission boards as the equals of male missionaries. Lottie Moon was an exception, of course, for she insisted on equal treatment and got it. This did not endear her to her fellow male missionaries and was not appreciated by Southern Baptist leaders. Since women missionaries in the field oftentimes functioned apart from others, they had opportunities to bend protocol and frequently did—without broadcasting that they had done so. The FMB almost certainly appreciated the work of their female appointees, single and married, but the board was not inclined to challenge the male chauvinism in the SBC, and women missionaries continued to be regarded primarily as assistants to men. Because of possible spin-off benefits from the Women's Liberation movement during the 1960s and 1970s, the convention and the FMB might have moved toward more equality for women missionaries during the 1980s, if the denomination had continued to be controlled by its traditional leaders. Those leaders, however, lost their hold on the convention during the 1980s, when the fundamentalist element of the denomination engineered a takeover from the old "moderate" contingent. Extremely conservative, the new leaders

---

[41] *Annual of the SBC* (1883) appendix B, I-V; Paper by Bentley, Baptist History Files, Women's Role in Church, Southern Baptist Historical Library and Archives, Nashville, TN.

interpreted the Bible literally, seizing upon a number of passages to put women back in their traditional, subordinate place.

How it would be for future women missionaries under the new fundamentalist leaders was made rather clear by the case of Greg and Katrina Pennington in 1986. This married couple served Northwest Baptist Church in Ardmore, Oklahoma—Greg as minister of education and Katrina as minister of preschool children. Because of Katrina's ordination by the church, the Enon Baptist Association withdrew fellowship from Northwest Baptist. Then, when the couple attempted to secure an appointment from the FMB to go as missionaries to Scotland, they were denied. Although North Carolina pastor Mark Corts, who was chairman of the FMB trustees, insisted that the rejection of the Penningtons had nothing to do with Katrina's ordination, the evidence suggested otherwise. Few people outside of fundamentalist Baptist circles believed Corts.[42]

By 1991 the fundamentalists completely dominated the SBC, and both before and since that year, they demonstrated quite plainly their views on gender. Politically and socially, Southern Baptist women had made gains because of changes that came about in society at large, but in the SBC of the year 2000 they were right back in the subordinate place they had occupied throughout more than a hundred and fifty years of denominational history. It is probably fair to say that women missionaries then being sent out by the SBC mission boards felt that equality with their brethren was at least as far from their reach as it had been in the days of Lottie Moon. In spite of all the splendid contributions that SBC women missionaries had made since the 1840s, their status remained essentially unchanged in the year 2000. In fact, retrogression on gender issues was the order of the day in the SBC after 1984 and,

---

[42] David T. Morgan, *The New Crusades, the New Holy Land: Conflict in the Southern Baptist Convention, 1969–1991* (Tuscaloosa and London: University of Alabama Press, 1996) 126, 157.

especially, after 1991, when women, whether laywomen or missionaries, were expected to submit to their husbands, eschew leadership roles in churches, and refrain from seeking ordination.

CHAPTER 5

"THROUGH THE SEA OF OPPOSITION"

WMU, A VEHICLE FOR PROVIDING SERVICE AND ACHIEVING STATUS

Catherine B. Allen, in her monumental history of the Woman's Missionary Union, observed in 1987 that the creation of a general woman's missionary organization by Southern Baptist women was dreaded by the SBC, but that the WMU "managed to baptize the Convention in a sea of prayer, a gush of funds, a stream of consciousness, and finally a watershed of social action." Not only did Southern Baptist men dread the formation of a general woman's organization inside the SBC, they put up numerous roadblocks to try to keep it from becoming a reality. Consequently, the formation of the WMU took years and was a matter of serious controversy, for at least some Southern Baptist men realized the impressive contributions women made to the denomination and contended with their more numerous brethren who loathed the thought of women organizing. Some of the more progressive brethren warned in 1885, three years before the WMU was formally established, that the woman question needed "careful handling." One noted, "Extreme views on one side or the other, indiscreet remarks, unwise action may do more harm than many years can repair. The good sisters have too much sense and are too much in earnest to be satisfied with flattering platitudes and empty compliments." Three years later, in 1888, after years of talking and planning, Southern Baptist women finally organized the Woman's Missionary Union as an "auxiliary" agency of the Southern Baptist Convention. Because most Southern Baptist men had rebuffed them, in spite of the large sums they had raised for missions, the women took it upon themselves to ignore male opposition and bring together their various state mission societies under one umbrella organization, thus giving Southern Baptist women the vehicle they needed to achieve their goals for missions in their own way.[1]

One of the few Southern Baptist men who supported the establishment of the WMU was a South Carolina pastor named John Stout. His wife, Fannie, delivered the keynote address at the foundational meeting in 1888, and in it, she said, "We do not desire a separate work, but if in some particulars we separate ourselves as women, it is that we may gather greater momentum with which to push forward our united work." She went on to add that the brethren were their guardians and would come around to supporting them when they realized that the women did not seek a radical new departure. Eventually, the WMU did gain approval to organize, but in order to do so, the organization had to declare that it did not intend to administer funds but to raise them and did not intend to appoint missionaries but to inform churches

---

[1] Catherine B. Allen, *A Century to Celebrate: History of Woman's Missionary Union* (Birmingham AL: Woman's Missionary Union, 1987) 9 ; Wayne Flynt and Gerald Berkley, *Taking Christianity to China: Alabama Missionaries in the Middle Kingdom, 1850–1950* (Tuscaloosa and London: University of Alabama Press, 1997) 201; Alma Hunt, *History of Woman's Missionary Union* (Nashville: Convention Press, 1964) 21, 26.

about them and pray for them. In others words, the women were to play an educational and supporting role only.[2]

Besides fearing that the women would take charge in the work of missions, some Southern Baptist men were deeply concerned about the women speaking publicly. The venerable John A. Broadus was careful to caution against "women speaking before promiscuous assemblies." He and others who shared his views insisted that women speak only to women and not to mixed groups. The first generation of WMU leaders accepted this view, believing it was scriptural for women to remain silent in the presence of men. Even Lottie Moon, who was considerably more assertive than the majority of the Southern Baptist women of her time, was reluctant for a very long time to speak before unconverted Chinese men. On the other hand, since the founders of the WMU were constantly reminded that they should not address men, they excluded men from their annual WMU meeting for many years.[3]

Some Southern Baptist men welcomed the new WMU, fully embracing it and looking to it gratefully for the help they knew it could and wanted to give. A few months after the organization came into being, Secretary Henry A. Tupper of the FMB went to Annie Armstrong, one of WMU's founders, and shared with her a letter from Lottie Moon. As usual, Moon was asking that Southern Baptists send more missionaries to China. Tupper told Armstrong that the only hope for China was "through the women" and asked that the WMU give special attention "to this matter." In just a few months the WMU raised $3,315.26, which was enough to send three single, missionary women to China.[4]

---

[2] William R. Estep, *Whole Gospel, Whole World: The Foreign Mission Board of the Southern Baptist Convention, 1845–1995* (Nashville: Broadman & Holman Publishers, 1995) 122; Hunt, *History of Woman's Missionary Union*, 29–30.

[3] Allen, *A Century to Celebrate*, 327–28.

[4] Hunt, *History of Woman's Missionary Union*, 44–45.

The women who founded the WMU were white and wealthy, from the Southern gentry and aristocracy. Along with women missionaries, the WMU leaders became role models for Southern Baptist women. Although those women were never militant in asserting the rights of women in their churches or in society, they were still more progressive than the average Southern Baptist woman. They did it quietly, but they did question the hidebound Southern culture and rigid Baptist custom that kept women silent and subservient. Over time, the WMU added to its ranks women from a variety of classes and races, thus achieving a union of minorities from diverse cultural backgrounds. But while they were increasingly aggressive, the women of the WMU were not militant. Some of them supported the suffragist movement early in the twentieth century and pushed for representation on denominational committees after World War I, but they were reluctant to endorse the Women's Liberation movement of the post-World War II years until 1970. The first WMU leader to meet the issue of women's rights head on in the post-World War II era was Executive Director Carolyn Weatherford, who in 1975 asked the denomination's Christian Life Commission to conduct a seminar on "Freedom for Christian Women." This seminar was followed by several "consultations" on women in church-related vocations.[5] While Weatherford and her successor, Dellana O'Brien, were bolder in pushing for the rights of Southern Baptist women than any WMU leaders had been before them, only extremists could view them as promoters of a radical feminist agenda. Like their sister leaders who preceded them, they sought to enhance women's status and to secure equality with men in denominational affairs, but they pushed for their objectives in a moderate fashion, not a militant one. Above all, they sought to maintain the independence of the WMU in carrying out its mission.

---

[5] Allen, *A Century to Celebrate*, 67–68, 325–26, 340–42.

To appreciate fully the great work that Southern Baptist women have accomplished through the WMU, it is necessary to know the story of that organization's founding and development. The WMU evolved over four decades and resulted from the scattered efforts of Southern Baptist women to obey the Great Commission of Jesus Christ to go into all the world and carry his gospel to every creature. So-called "missionary Baptists"—and Southern Baptists certainly identified themselves as such—had a passion for missions. They wanted to convert the heathen both at home and abroad—hence the early establishment of their Home Mission and Foreign Mission Boards. Yet, an interest in mission work on the part of Baptist women preceded the establishment of the Southern Baptist Convention in 1845. Local societies to raise money for charity and missions, both domestic and foreign, appeared in various parts of the South between 1813 and 1844. Sometimes called "mite societies," these women's groups were allowed, because of their monetary contributions, to appoint men delegates to the Triennial Convention, and sometime after the creation of the SBC, they were represented, again through male delegates, at annual conventions. In 1868, when the SBC met at the First Baptist Church of Baltimore, Ann Baker Graves, wife of physician John J. Graves of that city, called a meeting of Southern Baptist women so that she could report on the activities of Rosewell Graves, her physician son who was then serving as a missionary in Canton, China. Acting as both a physician and minister, Rosewell Graves trained Chinese women to be "Bible women," and sent them into Chinese households to tell Bible stories. Thus, it was Rosewell Graves's work that inspired this first general meeting of Southern Baptist women and motivated a number of sisters to organize societies in Maryland, South Carolina, Virginia, and Kentucky. Those societies promoted the plan of giving to missions through regular "mite box" contributions and holding regular prayer meetings to pray for missionaries. More Southern Baptist women took part each year.

Societies in Newberry, South Carolina, and Richmond, Virginia, assumed the responsibility of supporting Eddie Moon's work in China. The SBC's Foreign Mission Board saw the possibilities in the movement and supplied "mite boxes" to all Southern Baptist women who would receive them.[6]

In 1871 another significant step was taken by women when Ann Graves started a society called Woman's Mission to Woman. As the society's corresponding secretary she encouraged women all over the South to organize "for prayer and the dissemination of missionary intelligence." She sent out circular letters, urging women in each home to raise money by means of the mite boxes. The garnet-colored mite boxes used by the society had Woman's Mission to Woman written in gold letters on their side. Naturally, Graves focused much attention on the mission work in China because of her son, and she especially urged support for women missionaries to that country. She made it known that male missionaries could not help Chinese women, for those women could not have contact with any men outside their own families.[7]

Earnest Southern Baptist women had reason to be encouraged about the future of mission work in China and elsewhere when Henry A. Tupper became secretary of the FMB in 1872. He supported the women's efforts to promote missions and proposed a more active role for them to the annual meeting of the SBC that year.[8] Unfortunately, the denomination was not ready to listen, and Tupper backed away, choosing to move forward cautiously. The opposition against increasing women's activities and visibility is easily explained. Lurking in the backs

---

[6] William W. Barnes, *The Southern Baptist Convention, 1845–1953* (Nashville: Broadman Press, 1954) 141–43; Hunt, *History of Woman's Missionary Union*, 11–12.

[7] Estep, *Whole Gospel, Whole World*, 120; Hunt, *History of Woman's Missionary Union*, 12–13.

[8] Estep, *Whole Gospel, Whole World*, 120–21.

of the minds of Southern Baptist brethren were the Apostle Paul's words excluding women from playing a leading role in church affairs. There was also the question of what Southerners in general regarded as the unseemly and radical shenanigans of the activist women who were pushing women's rights in the North. A softening of attitude was still several years away.

Tupper kept nudging the brothers gently and gradually. In 1874 the FMB recommended formation of an executive or central committee for women's work in each state. At first these committees were appointed by the FMB in consultation with "judicious brethren," but in ten years they became self-perpetuating. Almost simultaneously with the recommendation of central committees by the FMB, John Stout assumed the pastorate of the Welsh Neck Baptist Church in South Carolina. He led his new church in establishing a Woman's Missionary Society. Louisa McIntosh was its first president, and her sister Martha soon became chairman of the South Carolina central committee. Using the method of the mite boxes for raising money, Martha soon had South Carolina leading the states in mission-giving.[9]

Convinced by the mid-1870s that state central committees were the key to promoting the mission enterprise, Henry Tupper went in 1876 to visit Fannie E. S. Heck at her home in Raleigh, North Carolina. Heck was destined to become one of the WMU's most outstanding national presidents in future years. The FMB secretary asked her to take charge of forming a statewide central committee in North Carolina to promote foreign missions. She agreed, but because of male opposition in the state convention, the central committee for North Carolina was stillborn in 1877. Even so, in that very year it was proposed at the annual meeting of the SBC that the convention appoint a south-wide "Central

---

[9] Barnes, *The Southern Baptist Convention*, 144; Hunt, *History of Woman's Missionary Union*, 14, 38.

Committee to combine their efforts, to stimulate the work, and give permanent record to their success." In other words, one central committee, according to the proposal, should be established for the denomination instead of simply having individual central committees in each state. Predictably there was strong opposition on theological and social grounds to such a committee, and the consensus view was in favor of continuing the various state organizations. Surprisingly, the FMB declared against one south-wide central committee in 1878, no doubt because Tupper sensed that there was too much opposition to it among the brethren or because he himself had misgivings about centralization. Consequently, at the annual convention in 1879 the Committee on Woman's Work recommended that women in all churches be urged to form missionary societies and that not one but two "Central Committees" (one for foreign missions and one for home missions) be appointed in each state. The various societies were to raise money and divide it between the two mission boards as they saw fit and report their activities to the central committees regularly. This plan was approved.[10]

Ann Graves, one of the most fervent advocates of women's mission work among the Southern Baptist sisters, died in 1878, and her mantle fell on feisty Sallie Rochester Ford of Kentucky. A fine writer and a bold journalist, Ford was not intimidated by male critics. She led Baptist women in promoting central committees in several states, beginning in 1883. Despite seeing women's work ignored by Baptist state conventions, she persisted in her work. In many instances pastors refused to supply the names of the women in their churches, not wanting them to serve on the central committees.[11]

---

[10] Catherine B. Allen, *Laborers Together with God: 22 Great Women in Baptist Life* (Birmingham AL: Woman's Missionary Union, 1987) 28; *Annual of the SBC* (1877): 22, 28, 59; (1879): 37; Barnes, *The Southern Baptist Convention*, 145; Hunt, *History of Woman's Missionary Union*, 16–18.

[11] Hunt, *History of Woman's Missionary Union*, 18–20.

The women had come too far by the early 1880s to be put
off any longer, and they pressed on, in spite of the attitude of
their husbands and pastors. In 1881 there were about 500
women's societies in the Southern states. From 350 of them
Henry Tupper received a report and over $6000 in contributions
to foreign missions that year. At the 1881 convention the Committee on Woman's Work recommended the formation of central committees in states that did not already have them. It
further recommended that the FMB, when it deemed it wise to do
so, appoint "some competent woman" as superintendent of
woman's work to collect the money for missions and disseminate
information to the societies. In the following year the HMB
rejoiced that "our churches are catching the spirit of the
Apostolic times" by being "more inclined to appreciate and
utilize woman's influence, gifts, and labors in the building up of
the churches and in the spread of the Gospel at home and
abroad." Of the 500 societies that had cooperated with the FMB
in 1881, only 31 had contributed to the HMB. It was understood
that the HMB would henceforth be more active in seeking the aid
of the women's mission societies.[12]

As women sought to become increasingly involved in the
mission enterprise, Southern Baptist men became more alarmed.
The women began in the early 1880s to single out biblical women
like Phoebe and Priscilla and praise them for the service
attributed to them in scripture. They constantly called attention
to the fact that in Asia women were not permitted to talk to
male missionaries. If those women were going to be reached,
women would have to reach them. As innocent as these
observations were to the ears of women, they prompted
apprehension in men. One Baptist pastor said that if women
really desired to help churches, they should sing louder in the
worship services! But the women persisted, and as they moved

---

[12] *Annual of the SBC* (1881): 22; and (1882): 25, 38.

closer to forming a "general committee" between 1884 and 1888, the controversy intensified. In 1884 a meeting of women called by the Woman's Mission to Woman met during the SBC's annual convention. Reports of twelve state central committees were read. It was noted that the number of women's mission societies had reached 642 and that the financial contributions by the women had increased by 68 percent over the year before. There was specific discussion about a national organization at this meeting.[13]

As the women moved closer to a national organization, the tension mounted. On the eve of the annual convention at Augusta in 1885 the women claimed the name Woman's Missionary Union of the Southern Baptist Convention, but in an apparent attempt to allay male apprehensions, it was noted in an article in *Heathen Helper* that "our work is not an independent one, but auxiliary to the convention." As the atmosphere became more electrified, the FMB sought to please the women and conservative Southern Baptist men at the same time. The board asked the SBC to *give* women fuller representation in the denomination before they demanded it. However, the men at the Augusta convention were in no mood to make concessions on the woman question, for that was the year the convention refused to seat as delegates Mary Oldham Eagle and Margaretta Dudgeon Early from Arkansas. In the end, the 1885 convention simply endorsed the status quo, leaving the mission work of the women to the central committees in the various states.[14]

---

[13] Allen, *A Century to Celebrate*, 36; Wayne Flynt, *Alabama Baptists: Southern Baptists in the Heart of Dixie* (Tuscaloosa and London: The University of Alabama Press, 1998) 175–76; Leon McBeth, "The Role of Women in Southern Baptist History," *Baptist History & Heritage* (January 1977): 25.

[14] Allen, *A Century to Celebrate*, 37–38; Hunt, *History of Woman's Missionary Union*, 21–22.

By 1887 Southern Baptist women who favored the establishment of a "general organization" were out of patience and determined to move forward. That year, representatives of the state central committees met in Louisville. More than 300 women were present at Broadway Methodist Church, and Sallie Ford presided at the meeting. Annie Armstrong offered resolutions calling for "organizing a general committee" and making clear that the women had no desire "to interfere with the management of the existing Boards of the Convention, either in the appointment of missionaries, or the direction of mission work." The "general organization" would merely collect money more efficiently and disseminate information. Armstrong's resolution included a request for each of the state central committees to appoint three women delegates to meet in Richmond the next year, simultaneously with the annual SBC convention, to decide the question of organizing nationally. All of this was announced that fall in the *Religious Herald*, the Virginia Baptist journal. There was considerable adverse criticism. The charge was made numerous times that such an organization would work in opposition to regular church programs, and the General Association of Virginia did not favor it.[15]

In spite of all the opposition, the women would not be denied any longer, but they did attempt to act in such a way as to lessen the men's hostility. For several years the spearheads for a national woman's organization had been Sallie Ford and Annie Armstrong. When time came for the foundational meeting in Richmond on 11 May 1888, Sallie Ford, a lightning rod who attracted conservative criticism, was not asked to preside. Instead, that honor went to Mrs. Theodore Whitfield, the wife of a pastor who had recently left North Carolina to take a pastorate in Richmond. Before the vote was taken on 14 May the timid

---

[15] Allen, *A Century to Celebrate*, 41; Barnes, *The Southern Baptist Convention*, 151–53; Hunt, *History of Woman's Missionary Union*, 25; Leon McBeth, *Women in Baptist Life* (Nashville: Broadman Press, 1979) 95.

Mrs. Whitfield, who wondered if the women should wait for the men's approval, asked to be relieved as presiding officer. Annie Armstrong stepped forward to lead the thirty-two delegates from twelve states to make the critical decision. In addition to the thirty-two delegates from twelve states, about a hundred women from Richmond were in attendance, plus women from Alabama and North Carolina who were not official delegates. Baptist leaders in Alabama had denied permission for the Alabama central committee to send delegates, as did the men in North Carolina.[16]

While the women deliberated for three days in a basement Sunday school room of the Broad Street Methodist Church, the annual meeting of the SBC was being held a block away in Richmond's First Baptist Church. Obviously news of what was happening at each meeting was finding its way to the other. At the convention one pastor expressed apprehension at what the women might be doing and reportedly said, "You never can tell what the women might take to praying for, if left alone." Fannie Heck, who was in Richmond to attend the women's meeting as an unofficial observer from North Carolina, said that while the women were deliberating, some men over at First Baptist claimed that "one thing would lead to another," if the women united their mission organizations. Finally, one delegate at the convention stood up and told the story of a woman sending her little girl to the spring to draw water. When the child did not return after a long while, the mother went to find her. She found the girl crying at the spring. When asked what was wrong, the little girl asked her mother what if she, the child, grew up, married, had a little girl, sent her to the spring, and she fell in and drowned? Upon finishing the story, the speaker said it seemed to him that the

---

[16] Allen, *A Century to Celebrate*, 41–46; *Annual of the SBC* (1895): appendix, 88; Barnes, *The Southern Baptist Convention*, 153–55; Flynt, *Alabama Baptists*, 174; Hunt, *History of Woman's Missionary Union*, 2–3, 28–29, 31–32, 34–35; McBeth, *Women in Baptist Life*, 96–97.

brethren were contemplating a lot of trouble.... He did not finish the sentence. After that, all objections were laughed away, and the convention adopted a report stating "that this Convention and all its officers and employees encourage the formation of women's missionary circles...for the double purpose of exciting interest in mission work and raising funds for the spread of the Gospel." Never again was there opposition on the floor of a convention to the women's mission work as such.[17]

As the men at the convention fussed and finally acquiesced in the formation of a national women's organization for missions, the women hemmed and hawed for three days before acting on 14 May. The keynote speaker, Fannie Stout of South Carolina, gave a stirring speech. After her address, Annie Armstrong pushed the issue of organization. Her motion to create a general organization was seconded by Fannie Breedlove Davis of Texas. The roll was called amidst tension and murmuring. Armstrong spoke up and said that Maryland voted yes. Nine other states followed with an affirmative vote, while Mississippi abstained, as did Virginia, to await the approval of the men. Though not a delegate, Fannie Heck spoke up and said that under the circumstances, her state would have to wait. In spite of the ten votes for organization, some still debated whether it would be best to wait for the men to approve. Indignantly, Annie Armstrong asked, "Is it our work or not?" Fannie Davis had already made her position clear, declaring, "This movement is not for 'woman's rights,' though we have our rights, the highest of which is the right for service." Thus, ten states—Maryland, South Carolina, Missouri, Tennessee, Texas, Arkansas, Florida, Georgia, Louisiana, and Kentucky—became the constituting states. Mississippi, Alabama, North Carolina, and Virginia would join shortly, although there was a dramatic development with

---

[17] Barnes, *The Southern Baptist Convention*, 155; Fannie E. S. Heck, *In Royal Service: The Mission Work of Southern Baptist Women* (Richmond: Foreign Mission Board, 1913) 132–33.

regard to Alabama. Two months after the Richmond convention the Alabama Baptist Convention met in Talladega, and the angry male delegates at that meeting tabled the women's report and abolished the state central committee. A year later, however, that ill-advised action was rescinded, and Alabama did join the new WMU.[18]

The original name of the new organization was the Executive Committee of Woman's Mission Societies, Auxiliary to the Southern Baptist Convention. In 1890 it was changed, at the suggestion of Mrs. Stainback Wilson of Georgia, to what it has been ever since—Woman's Missionary Union, Auxiliary to the Southern Baptist Convention. Its headquarters was to be in Baltimore, and its first officers were Martha E. McIntosh (president), Annie Armstrong (corresponding secretary), Mrs. James Pollard (recording secretary), and Mrs. John Pullen (treasurer). Miss McIntosh was from South Carolina, while the other three were all from Baltimore. The WMU's first president was the youngest of eight children. She was born at Society Hill, South Carolina, and brought up in the Welsh Neck Baptist Church. John H. McIntosh, her father, was a wealthy merchant and planter. "Mattie," as Martha's family called her, grew up dreaming of being a foreign missionary, but she failed to pursue the dream because of a tendency toward tuberculosis among the McIntoshes. As the newly minted president of the WMU Martha probably had no illusions about who was in charge of the new organization over which she nominally presided. It was the corresponding secretary, not the president, who would direct the organization. For eighteen years Armstrong ruled the roost at the WMU, and the only president who challenged her dictatorial

---

[18] Allen, *A Century to Celebrate*, 44–46; Flynt, *Alabama Baptists*, 174, 176; Hunt, *History of Woman's Missionary Union*, 31–32.

ways was Fannie Heck, who precipitated a feud with the corresponding secretary that went on for at least five years.[19]

Annie Armstrong was, for all practical purposes, the heart and soul of the WMU during its early years, and the only name that eclipses hers in the whole history of the SBC is Lottie Moon's. In a sense, these two women were the co-founders of the WMU, since Moon urged for years from her mission post in Shantung Province that Southern Baptist women unite in one organization to promote missions more effectively. There is clear evidence that Armstrong was inspired to act because of Lottie Moon's admonitions. Not only did Armstrong force the issue of organization at Richmond in 1888, the WMU constitution, which was adopted there, was primarily the work of Annie and her sister Alice. The document's preamble disclaimed "all intention of independent action" and proposed to collect funds "to be disbursed by the Boards of the Southern Baptist Convention." Besides helping to write the foundational document of the WMU, Armstrong saw to it that the organization's headquarters was in her hometown. The WMU accepted quarters that were offered rent-free by the Maryland Baptist Union. Called the "Mission Room," the headquarters was a combination of office, library, and reading room that had been used by the women's missionary societies of Baltimore since 1886. Since Annie was born into a wealthy family, she could afford to serve the WMU without pay, which she did for many years.[20]

In some ways Annie Armstrong was a conservative Southern Baptist male's dream woman. She took Paul's admonitions against women speaking in the church in the most literal sense. In her mind, women were not supposed to speak in mixed assemblies or usurp any authority that the Bible assigned to men.

---

[19] Barnes, *The Southern Baptist Convention*, 153–55; Hunt, *History of Woman's Missionary Union*, vii-viii, 2–3, 34–35, 37–38, 54–56.

[20] Barnes, *The Southern Baptist Convention*, 156; Hunt, *History of Woman's Missionary Union*, 39–41; McBeth, *Women in Baptist Life*, 96–97.

She was careful always to insist that the WMU was in no way independent of the SBC. On the other hand, Armstrong could be irascible and intransigent. For instance, she got into a quarrel with Henry Tupper when he tried to dictate how the money raised by the WMU would be used by the FMB. In 1890 Armstrong insisted that some money raised by the WMU be used to build a chapel in Rio de Janeiro, and she pushed until she had her way. This created a rift between her and Tupper, and henceforth she was compelled to work through T. P. Bell, Tupper's assistant, and John Pollard, the chairman of the FMB's Committee on Woman's Work. Strong-willed though she was when she was convinced that she was operating in her proper sphere, Armstrong gave the WMU able leadership and contributed mightily to the cause of Southern Baptist missions. Denominational leaders praised her highly when she resigned in 1906, and since she did not die until 1938, she lived to see the Home Mission Offering, taken in Southern Baptist churches at Easter, named in her honor.[21]

Although born in an atmosphere of controversy and scorned by many Southern Baptist men, the WMU proved a godsend to the SBC. In less than a decade perceptive and moderate Southern Baptist men were fully aware that the women were doing far more than their share in the work of the denomination. In 1892 James B. Gambrell, at that juncture from Mississippi, gave a report on Woman's Work, and it clearly demonstrated that the amounts of money flowing from the WMU to the FMB and the HMB had increased dramatically each year over the previous five years. Even so, there was still that hang-up regarding a woman's place, for the committee urged "the expansion of woman's work to the utmost *within scriptural limitations*."[22] Again in 1893 a convention report praised the WMU for its monetary

---

[21] Allen, *A Century to Celebrate*, 330; Allen, *Laborers Together with God*, 172–173; Estep, *Whole Gospel, Whole World*, 136–137.

[22] Emphasis added.

contributions and noted that all signs indicated tremendous success with the organization's plans for expanding and increasing contributions. At the 1894 convention John Stout, one of the very earliest supporters of the women's cause in the SBC, read the report on Woman's Work, as follows: "The Woman's Missionary Union works entirely under the direction of the two Mission Boards. It undertakes only what those Boards want done by it. It seems important to emphasize this. 'The Woman's Mission work is not, and those in charge do not wish it to be, independent work; they are the servants of this Convention.'" Obviously the brethren had to be reassured constantly that the women would not veer from their self-imposed auxiliary status. After discussion, the report was approved, and sometime after that the women lost a true friend, for John Stout died before leaving the convention.[23]

In 1895, on the fiftieth anniversary of the SBC, W. H. Whitsitt, perhaps the greatest of early Southern Baptist historians, delivered his "Historical Discourse on the Fiftieth Anniversary of the Southern Baptist Convention" at the annual meeting in Dallas. He put the WMU matter in proper perspective when he said: "There were many obstacles and many opponents, but in the year 1888, was finally established the Woman's Missionary Union, with its seat in Baltimore. From the outset the women have been exceedingly helpful, but since the establishment of the Central Board, they have become, in several important respects, the right arm of our power." Additional praise was heaped upon the WMU at the 1896 convention in a report that included the words, "In no department of our work has there been a more rapid increase in receipts or a more hopeful and permanent development along all lines of missionary enterprise."[24]

---

[23] *Annual of the SBC* (1892): 31–32; (1893): 26–27; (1894): 28–29; (1895) appendix, 89.

[24] *Annual of the SBC* (1895): appendix, 88; and (1896): 30.

By any and all measuring sticks the WMU, in less than ten years, had produced the goods for SBC missions. Yet, its members could not serve as delegates to the annual conventions and had no representation on SBC boards or committees. Women could not address the annual meetings of the SBC or the yearly meetings of the state conventions. To keep peace, they had to sit in silence when the reports of their own work were read by men. Undaunted at being regarded as second-class members of their denomination, they pressed forward and expanded their work. Quite early they attached themselves to the Baptist World Alliance (BWA), which held its first congress at London in 1904. At the fledgling organization's second congress in Philadelphia, Fannie Heck was a speaker, and other WMU women participated as well. As a result of participating in the BWA, the WMU began extending its organization to other countries—Brazil in 1908, Cuba in 1913, Nigeria and Mexico in 1919, and Japan in 1920. In just a few years the WMU organized nationwide in fifty-eight countries. By this time the WMU had a new leader, Kathleen Mallory from Alabama. No doubt with Mallory's blessing and probably her assistance, Jessie Stakely, the national president from Montgomery, Alabama, helped relocate the WMU's national headquarters from Baltimore to Birmingham in 1921. Growth and expansion continued for the organization at its new home, as its membership passed a half million in 1929 and a million in the 1950s. Its membership started to decline, however, after 1963, its peak year, when women began to move into the workplace in increasing numbers. Membership reached a plateau in 1974 and remained fairly stable during the last quarter of the twentieth century.[25]

As the WMU grew and prospered it made innumerable contributions to the denomination and society. Of course, the

---

[25] Allen, *A Century to Celebrate*, 84–86, 88, 90; Flynt, *Alabama Baptists*, 133; Hunt, *History of Woman's Missionary Union*, 163.

two most successful and highly publicized efforts of the WMU over many decades have been the Lottie Moon Christmas Offering for foreign missions and the Annie Armstrong Easter Offering for home missions. Between 1888 and 1987 the WMU contributed over $1 billion to SBC causes, and that fact reveals only part of the story. By 1999 the WMU had given nearly $1.3 billion through the Lottie Moon Christmas Offering alone. Giving such impressive sums were Southern Baptist women who were relatively poor, for they did not control the wealth of their household or their society. Yet, they gave more generously than Southern Baptists in general. In 1936 a study of twenty leading denominations by the United Stewardship Council reported that Southern Baptist per capita giving to missions, education, and benevolence was only $1.87, the lowest among the denominations. But, when the WMU was studied separately from the rest of Southern Baptists, the per capita figure climbed to $4.49.[26] There seems to be clear justification for concluding that the women were carrying a disproportionate share of the financial load among Southern Baptists.

While some Southern Baptist agencies regularly fell into debt, the WMU was careful to ward off the intrusion of red ink. Consequently, the organization was sometimes summoned to the financial rescue of agencies like the FMB and the HMB. For example, in 1932, during the depths of the Great Depression, both mission boards were deeply in debt. They reported that they could not make it through the summer without help. An emergency SBC offering was taken that summer, bringing in $204,000, of which the WMU gave $52,000. This was not enough, for the depression worsened, and by 1933 the FMB and the HMB together had an indebtedness of $3 million. The WMU responded by using surplus funds from the Lottie Moon

---

[26] Allen, *A Century to Celebrate*, 116, 141, 147–160; Estep, *Whole Gospel, Whole World*, 393.

Christmas Offering of that year to underwrite the salaries of some missionaries on furlough so that they could return to their mission fields and to pay the "outgoing expenses" of eight new missionaries who were to be sent out after the SBC meeting of 1934. Thus, in one of the most difficult periods ever faced by the FMB, it was the WMU that offered the necessary helping hand.[27]

From the very beginning of the WMU's existence some men who were critical of the organization did not mind asking it for funds. When the SBC voted at Birmingham in 1891 to celebrate the one hundredth anniversary of William Carey's going to India as a missionary, T. T. Eaton of Kentucky was named chairman of the Centennial Committee. Eaton went over to the annual meeting of the WMU and asked the women to support the centennial celebration He asked them to raise $250,000, a sum that would be used equally by the FMB and the HMB for chapel buildings, Bible translation, and publication work. Turned off by Eaton's approach, the women reacted negatively at first. It was said that "a slight breeze ruffled the placid calmness." When Eaton read the Centennial Committee's resolution, one woman noted that this was "*Woman's* Missionary Union," and it did not need gentlemen to frame its resolutions. Another reportedly said, "I think we should appoint a delegate to that [SBC] convention." This was perhaps the first time that the women reacted adversely to "masculine chirography." In spite of being miffed at Eaton's style, the women contributed generously to the effort.[28]

Sometimes the WMU took the initiative in reviving defunct SBC causes. In 1883 the HMB had attempted unsuccessfully to establish the Church Building Loan Fund. Annie Armstrong resurrected the idea and succeeded where the HMB had failed.

---

[27] Allen, *A Century to Celebrate*, 129–32; Estep, *Whole Gospel, Whole World*, 231.

[28] Allen, *A Century to Celebrate*, 122; Hunt, *History of Woman's Missionary Union*, 49–50.

Begun in 1900 the fund had no assets, other than those raised by the WMU, until 1909. Between 1914–1915 the HMB sought to expand the fund by proclaiming a million dollar campaign. The WMU's goal was $225,000. Various efforts caused the fund to grow over the years, and by 1986 it had over $90 million in it. About the same time that the HMB began to enhance the fund, an official of the agency estimated that the WMU, with 7.6 percent of the SBC's membership, was giving 30.6 percent of all the money for home and foreign missions, not including what it gave for state and local missions.[29]

Indeed, the WMU gave vital support to every SBC fundraising campaign for decades. First came the Education Campaign of 1917, the goal of which was $15 million for Southern Baptist schools. Then, in 1919, came the highly ambitious Seventy-five Million Campaign, by which the SBC intended to raise $75 million over a five-year period. The SBC in 1920 named two women, Minnie Kennedy James and Kathleen Mallory (president and executive secretary respectively of the WMU), to sit on a convention committee—the very important committee that was to direct the Seventy-five Million Campaign. Although the denomination fell short of its goal by $17 million, the WMU raised $25,000 more than its assigned quota of $15 million.[30]

The WMU's success in raising money brought its members a measure of recognition by the brethren, and in 1923 when the large Committee on Future Program was appointed, it included a WMU officer from every state, as well as the organization's national president. One-third of the committee consisted of women, the highest percentage of women on an SBC-appointed committee before or since. This committee produced plans for the Cooperative Program, which began its existence at the 1925

---

[29] Allen, *A Century to Celebrate*, 120, 123–24.

[30] Ibid. 125–129; McBeth, "The Role of Women in Southern Baptist History," 20.

annual meeting of the SBC. In retrospect it is clear that this was one of the most significant steps ever taken by the denomination, but at the time it was not emphasized because of the theological quarrels that led to the adoption of the Baptist Faith and Message Statement of 1925. The WMU advocated what was known as the 50-50 principle, meaning that the money sent by the local churches to their respective state conventions would be divided equally between the state conventions and the national convention. Although this did not work out in actual practice, since the distribution is different from state to state, the WMU fully supported the Cooperative Program (CP), and it became the financial apparatus through which the SBC funds all of its agencies and activities. The CP has been an enormous success. One of its early significant achievements was that of helping the SBC get out of debt by 1943.[31]

Even though the WMU supported the CP, there were clashes when the SBC wanted the Lottie Moon Christmas Offering and the Annie Armstrong Easter Offering counted as part of the FMB and HMB's CP allocation. The WMU insisted that the two offerings be recognized as separate and apart from the CP allocation. For this, the WMU was shut out of the CP planning process, and for years the SBC Executive Committee refused to identify separately the money received from the two WMU offerings. This was an obvious attempt to downplay the two offerings in order to heap accolades on the Cooperative Program. One is hard pressed to know why, but the WMU continued to give its support to the CP.[32]

With the onset of the fundamentalist takeover of the SBC in the 1980s, trouble emerged again between the denomination and the WMU over the CP. In 1980 a Cooperative Program

---

[31] Allen, *A Century to Celebrate*, 133–34; Hunt, *History of Woman's Missionary Union*, 135; McBeth, "The Role of Women in Southern Baptist History," 20.

[32] Allen, *A Century to Celebrate*, 135–38.

Study Team was appointed by the SBC Executive Committee. The team was to study giving practices among Southern Baptists and to recommend a plan for increasing the offerings in the local churches and through the local churches to the cooperative ministries of the denomination. Carolyn Weatherford, executive director of the WMU, and Christine Gregory, WMU's national president, were on the team, which met periodically for three years. It was proposed in committee that the Lottie Moon Christmas Offering and the Annie Armstrong Easter Offering be factored into the CP, with the goals set by the SBC on recommendation from the WMU. There was no way the WMU would support such a proposal, so the team bypassed Weatherford and Gregory and submitted a plan called Planned Growth in Giving to the SBC. Needless to say, the women were offended.[33] From this time on, relations between the WMU and the new fundamentalist leaders of the denomination deteriorated.

In addition to raising far more money than its share for SBC causes and agencies, the WMU contributed in so many other ways, including the establishment of lasting institutions, the creation of significant organizations within the denomination, and the implementation of new church practices and ministries. In 1905 the WMU founded the Margaret Home in Greenville, South Carolina for the children of missionaries so that they could live and be educated in the United States while their parents were serving on faraway mission fields. When the home closed in 1913, the money that had been raised to support it became the Margaret Fund, to be used to help the children of missionaries pay their college expenses.[34]

Another educational effort by the WMU came in 1907 with the founding of the Woman's Missionary Union Training School, which was finally established after years of opposition.

---

[33] Ibid., 145.

[34] Barnes, *The Southern Baptist Convention*, 164; Hunt, *History of Woman's Missionary Union*, 68–70; McBeth, *Women in Baptist Life*, 126–27.

As early as 1895 some Texas women attempted to have a female missionary training school put on the SBC agenda. Not all of the resistance that emerged came from men, for Eliza Broadus, daughter of John A. Broadus, criticized Mina Everett, the leader of the Texas women, by asking, "Do you want to make preachers of our southern girls?" Another advocate of the school for women missionaries was E. Z. Simmons, a missionary to China for forty-two years. At the turn of the century he took up the cause, and a six-year struggle ensued within the WMU between those who favored the school and those who opposed it. Annie Armstrong, who, like Eliza Broadus, feared the school would turn women into preachers, vigorously opposed creating the institution. Fannie Heck, on the other hand, favored it, and when she was elected to an unprecedented third term as WMU president in 1906, the way was paved for the school to be founded in 1907. It was to be established in conjunction with Southern Seminary in Louisville. Prominent faculty members E. Y. Mullins and W. O. Carver were among the men at the seminary who favored the school. Quite a few women in the WMU showed their conservative colors during the controversy over the school's founding. For instance, Lillie Easterby Barker, who was WMU president from 1903 to 1906, submitted her resignation as president, following the lead of Annie Armstrong, who tendered hers as corresponding secretary. With women delegates from the WMU on the convention floor for the first time in 1907, the SBC voted to approve the school's founding, and the WMU soon organized it. It was to be "distinct from, but affiliated with, the Southern Seminary." The school's first building was purchased in 1912. By the early 1960s the name WMU Training School had been changed to Carver School of Missions and Social Work in honor of Professor W. O. Carver, who had strongly supported the institution. In 1963 the school's status changed when it was joined to Southern Seminary in order to gain accreditation.[35] The Carver School, as it came to be called by Southern Seminary students, enjoyed a reputation for educational excellence for several decades, but in the late 1990s it fell victim to fundamentalist hostility, when Al Mohler, Southern Seminary's young, doctrinaire president, led his institution to jettison the school over the issue of women's ordination.

In almost countless ways the WMU contributed to the enrichment and expansion of Southern Baptist life. In 1896, at the request of the FMB, it took charge of the "Sunbeam Bands" to train children in mission work and followed that up with the creation in 1907 of Royal Ambassadors for Southern Baptist boys, the Young Woman's Auxiliary the same year, and the Girls' Auxiliary (known as Acteens after 1970) in 1913. All of these groups engaged in mission study. Soon after again being elected president of the WMU in 1906, Fannie Heck launched *Our Mission Fields,* the first WMU periodical. In 1914 the name of the organ was changed to *Royal Service* and became a monthly publication instead of a quarterly one. Moreover, the WMU started or helped to start Vacation Bible School, the promotion of tithing, the hiring of African-Americans for professional positions, camping as a means of religious education, an annual week of prayer for foreign and home missions, a systematic

---

[35] Allen, *A Century to Celebrate,* 263–69, 278–81; Allen *Laborers Together with God,* 54–55; Barnes, *The Southern Baptist Convention,* 163–64; Hunt, *History of Woman's Missionary Union,* 70–81, 87–89; McBeth, *Women in Baptist Life,* 128. The most recent study of the Woman's Missionary Union Training School during its earliest years is T. Laine Scales, *All That Fits a Woman: Training Southern Baptist Women for Charity and Mission, 1907–1926* (Macon GA: Mercer University Press, 2000). For the material covered here see 15, 59, 69–84.

prayer plan for daily devotions, and women speaking at SBC meetings and holding denominational offices.[36]

Just as the WMU helped move the SBC forward, it did the same in society at large. While the WMU as an organization was never out front in the movement for woman's suffrage in the early part of the twentieth century, it played a far more progressive role in the matter of race relations. As early as 1944 a WMU committee recommended that the organization challenge the status quo in the area of race relations. Executive Secretary Kathleen Mallory was so alarmed by the recommendation that she sealed the committee's report in a vault. The next president of the WMU was Olive Martin of Virginia, a woman who would preside over the organization from 1945 to 1956 and who would push for better race relations. Sympathetic to blacks, Martin spoke often at African-American churches. Another leader in this area was Mildred Dodson McMurry, who joined the WMU staff in 1951. Twenty-one years earlier, at the 1930 annual meeting of the WMU, McMurry sounded the call for racial justice. In 1954, when the United States Supreme Court ordered the end of racial segregation in the public schools, the WMU endorsed the decision. McMurry became a member of the mayor of Birmingham's committee that was named to deal with the Supreme Court's desegregation order. Southern whites reacted with hostility to the WMU's stance in favor of integration, but the WMU courageously refused to budge. By this time Alma Hunt was the executive director, and she was angered when her own church in Birmingham, Southside Baptist, voted not to seat blacks. She was so upset by the vote

---

[36] Allen, *A Century to Celebrate*, 359; Allen, *Laborers Together with God*, 32–33; *Annual of the SBC* (1891): appendix A, II and III; Paper by Bentley, Baptist History Files, Women's Role in Church, Southern Baptist Historical Library and Archives, Nashville, TN, 8; Barnes, *The Southern Baptist Convention*, 159–61; Hunt, *History of Woman's Missionary Union*, 98; McBeth, *Women in Baptist Life*, 126.

that she refused to return to church for three weeks. Under her leadership the WMU continued to confront the racial issue by promoting classes to study T. B. Maston's *The Bible and Race,* a book that advocated a progressive position in racial matters.[37]

WMU women in the 1960s and 1970s began taking progressive stands on other issues besides race. For six years, 1975–1981, Christine Gregory presided over the WMU. In her first years as president she was confronted by questions about abortion and the ordination of women. On abortion she said that she was personally against it as a method of birth control, but she refused to go further than that, implying that there were possible circumstances under which women were justified in choosing abortion. As for ordination, she took her stand on two traditional Baptist doctrines—competency of the individual believer to make his or her own decisions after considering scriptural teaching and local church autonomy. To her the ordination of women was a matter for a particular woman and her local church to decide.[38] Oddly enough, Gregory's stand was considered a *"liberal"* one at the time. The subsequent coming to power of SBC fundamentalists made her position of 1975 more than "liberal"—it was anathema.

The WMU is a remarkable organization, and it has to its credit a vast number of achievements that are admirable by anyone's reckoning. Obviously, all of this could never have happened without some dynamic leadership. The WMU has been blessed from its origins in 1888 to the year 2000 by strong executive leadership in the persons of its presidents and its full-time executive officers, who have been called by a variety of

---

[37] Allen, *A Century to Celebrate,* 211–14, 234–35, 241–56; Allen, *Laborers Together with God,* 87; Alma Hunt, *Reflections From Alma Hunt* (Birmingham: Woman's Missionary Union, 1987) 71; Jesse C. Fletcher, *The Southern Baptist Convention: A Sesquicentennial History* (Nashville: Broadman & Holman Publishers, 1994) 173, 200.

[38] Allen, *Laborers Together with God,* 139.

names from corresponding secretary in the days of Annie Armstrong to executive director since the administration of Carolyn Weatherford. While all the presidents have been honorable women and worthy of note, some of them stand out more than others as strong leaders. In 1987 Catherine B. Allen, Lottie Moon's biographer and historian of the WMU, published a book about the most significant women in Baptist life, including the WMU's first fifteen presidents, its first five chief executive officers, plus Ann Baker Graves, Sallie Rochester Ford, and Lottie Moon. A few of the women she terms "great" deserve special mention in this study because they made it a point to stand up to the brethren in an effort to enhance the status of Southern Baptist women.

Abby Manly Gwathmey, WMU president for 1894–1895, was the organization's third president. The daughter of Basil Manly, Sr., prominent Alabama Baptist pastor and president of the University of Alabama, Abby was no avowed crusader for women's rights, but she did dare to use her own name instead of her husband's, and she was the only married WMU president until the 1970s who did so. Even Minnie Kennedy James, Ethlene Boone Cox, and Marie Wiley Mathis, none of them ever a shrinking violet, acted officially as Mrs. William Carey James, Mrs. W. J. Cox, and Mrs. R. L. Mathis respectively. Whether Mrs. William Henry Gwathmey meant to make a statement by officially acting as Abby Manly Gwathmey is not known, but her decision to do so was most unusual for the time and took at least a measure of courage.[39]

The WMU's first truly strong president, and as confrontational a one as the organization has ever had, was never faced with the choice of using her own name or her husband's. She had no husband during the fifty-three years she spent on earth. Fannie Exile Scudder Heck of Raleigh, North Carolina,

---

[39] Ibid., 39.

remains the only woman ever to be elected WMU president three different times, serving a total of fourteen years. It is likely that she would have served consecutive terms for more than two decades, if she had not clashed with Annie Armstrong. The battle of the spinsters began in 1894 over the role of president as stated in the WMU constitution. Heck refused to be a figurehead or, as she put it, to hold a "nominal position." On 26 March 1894, she said in a letter to Armstrong, "All during the last year it has been painfully borne in upon me that I was holding an office that I was not for many reasons filling." Returning to office after the term of Abby Manly Gwathmey in 1895, Heck withdrew again in 1899 as part of a peace agreement with Armstrong. Although she announced that she would decline reelection as president that year, she was elected anyway. She refused to serve again until 1906, when Armstrong announced her intention of resigning as corresponding secretary.[40]

Described by many as the most beautiful woman among Southern Baptists, Fannie Heck gave the WMU powerful leadership and led it to accomplish so much that she became renowned in all Baptist circles, not just those of Southern Baptists. She was a noted writer, writing columns in the publications of the FMB and the HMB and editing *Missionary Talks* in her own state of North Carolina. She wrote leaflets, books, and even poetry. She became a leader among Northern Baptist, as well as Southern Baptist, women. Unlike Annie Armstrong, who shrank from speaking in the presence of men, Heck gave a major speech at the Baptist World Alliance in 1911. She was president of the WMU during its twenty-fifth anniversary in 1913, when a massive fundraising drive was undertaken on behalf of the FMB and the HMB. Because of this effort, the WMU gained permission to report directly to the SBC

---

[40] Ibid., 31–32; Fletcher, *The Southern Baptist Convention*, 103–104; Hunt, *History of Woman's Missionary Union*, 51–54.

instead of *through* the mission boards, as had been customary up to that time. By 1915 the WMU, as a consequence of Heck's leadership, had established the Woman's Missionary Union Training School and sponsored missions study courses for women and young people. Local WMU groups also organized Girls Auxiliaries and Royal Ambassadors in various churches. *Royal Service,* the WMU publication that she had launched, had 19,000 subscribers. Moreover, the WMU had 250,000 members, worked with 13,424 affiliated organizations, and had given well over $300,000 to missions. The Committee on Woman's Work gave a glowing report on the success of the WMU at the annual convention in 1915.[41]

That was the year of Fannie Heck's death. It came on 25 August, four months after she had been unanimously reelected as WMU president—even though she had declined the nomination because of a terminal illness—presumably cancer. Following her death, the FMB entered a tribute to her in its minutes: "This generation has not been blessed with a better example of the womanhood which the New Testament exalts.... She exhibited a rare harmony of piety and strength, passion and fine sanity, delicate feminine modesty and strong leadership. Many will be under the spell of her life and devote themselves to her ideals."[42]

One of those who was long under the spell of Fannie Heck's life was her close friend, Minnie Kennedy James, who served as WMU president from 1916 to 1925. Minnie's husband, W. C. James, was a true friend of the WMU and of women's work in general. The year that his wife became president, James was asked to present the WMU report at the annual convention of the SBC. Minnie James was so fascinated with the peerless Fannie

---

[41] Allen, *Laborers Together with God*, 33; *Annual of the SBC* (1915): 30; Estep, *Whole Gospel, Whole World*, 194–96; Hunt, *History of Woman's Missionary Union*, 53–54.

[42] Allen, *Laborers Together with God*, 33, 36; Hunt, *History of Woman's Missionary Union*, 101.

Heck that she wrote her biography in 1939. Meanwhile, she demonstrated that she had learned a few lessons regarding assertiveness from her illustrious predecessor. Minnie went beyond simply following the example of Fannie Heck. Because of her own forceful leadership the stock of the WMU rose precipitously in the SBC during her presidency. She used her many accomplishments as leverage to seek equal treatment for women in the denomination. Women secured the right to vote at the annual convention during her tenure, and she demanded that women be given equal representation on SBC boards. She took as strong a stand for women's rights as any WMU officer ever has.[43]

As a result of James's assertive spirit, she and Kathleen Mallory, then the corresponding/executive secretary, became the first WMU officers to sit at a conference table with male leaders of the SBC. The WMU was asked to assist in the Seventy-five Million Campaign, and it met its goal of one-fifth of the total campaign. Next, the SBC went to work to establish the Cooperative Program, and James endorsed and assisted in that effort as well. She turned out to be one of the WMU's most effective presidents and perhaps its most persistent in pushing for women's equality.[44]

Succeeding Minnie Kennedy James as president of the WMU was another impressive leader, one who was mentioned earlier as the first woman to address an annual meeting of the SBC in 1929. She was Ethlene Boone Cox, who served as president from 1925 to1933. Perhaps no other woman in the history of the WMU has ever approached Cox as a speaker. Of her, Alma Hunt said, "There was deep and inspiring content in her words. She was a scholar and had the gift of beautiful communication, choice of words, quotations, voice, and handwriting." Praise was heaped

---

[43] Allen, *Laborers Together with God*, 59–61.
[44] Ibid.

upon her, too, by outsiders, as one reporter who heard her speak, wrote, "She has a clear musical voice that easily carries to the utmost limits of any ordinary auditorium. Her dignified, yet easy, manner, scintillating mind, her deep pious spirit, thoroughly captivated her audience.... You must hear her to appreciate her fully." As an author, Cox was also impressive, writing two books—*Star Trails* (1926), which was a compilation of her vespers messages to young women, and *Following in His Train* (1938), which was the fiftieth anniversary history of the WMU.[45]

This tall, fair, brown-eyed beauty was the first WMU president whose husband was a layman, but she did not shrink from bravely confronting the old-fashioned views of Southern Baptist ministers. Even as late as her presidency, many Southern Baptist preachers were firmly convinced that women should not address mixed audiences. She spoke rather forthrightly and with great effect at the 1929 convention, and she actually preached at Southside Baptist Church in Birmingham on 14 May 1931. She was thus the first WMU president to speak from a Baptist pulpit during a Sunday morning worship service. In 1939 this remarkable woman addressed a stadium crowd of 47,000 at the Baptist World Alliance in Atlanta. Before she spoke, a breeze scattered her notes, and the prince of Southern Baptist preachers, George W. Truett, attempted to pick them up. Cox reportedly waved her hand and said, "*Gone with the Wind.*" Eleven years earlier she had become the first woman named to the Baptist World Alliance executive committee.[46]

Doubtlessly this impressive woman could have remained president of the WMU for many more years, but her husband's heart problems caused her to give it up and take the job as treasurer of the organization. This was a paid position, and she

---

[45] Allen, *A Century to Celebrate*, 334; Allen, *Laborers Together with God*, 72; Hunt, *Reflections*, 18.

[46] Allen, *Laborers Together With God*, 66–72.

needed the money, as her husband died in 1934. Although Ethlene Boone Cox was never as straightforward as Minnie Kennedy James in pushing for women's rights, she assumed that women had rights in the SBC and she never hesitated in exercising them.[47]

Minnie James and Ethlene Cox set an example that most of their successors followed. Laura Armstrong, president from 1933 to 1945, was Cox's immediate successor, and she had already demonstrated her assertiveness in denominational affairs. In 1927 she and Annie Newton Thompson had become the first two women ever elected to the SBC's Executive Committee, and Armstrong remained on it until her death in 1945, more than half of those eighteen years as the only female member. In 1936 she presided over a joint meeting of Northern Baptists and Southern Baptists and thus became the first Southern Baptist woman to wield a gavel in front of Southern Baptist men. Armstrong did not mind calling attention to the fact that Southern Baptist men had a hang-up about putting women on SBC boards, and twice during her tenure as WMU president she thwarted efforts to change the status of the WMU. Olive Martin, who succeeded Armstrong, also displayed traits of strong leadership. She, as Armstrong had, fought to maintain the WMU's status as an auxiliary of the SBC, and she clashed on occasion with the FMB and HMB on how Lottie Moon and Annie Armstrong funds were to be allotted.[48]

In 1956 Martin was succeeded by Marie Mathis, who in 1963 would become the first woman to be elected to an SBC office. She was elected second vice-president of the convention. Nine years later, in 1972, she was nominated by prominent pastor Russell Dilday for the denomination's presidency, but she did not win the election. Still, Mathis remains the only woman

---

[47] Ibid.
[48] Ibid., 78, 80–81, 94–96.

who has ever been nominated for that prestigious office. A strong woman with a commanding presence, she served with the brethren on many important convention committees, and she was enough at ease when tension erupted that she sometimes "told the boys that she would 'clean their plows' if they didn't behave." Mathis had many firsts to her credit. One of the most noteworthy is that she was the first woman ever to deliver a commencement address at Southern Seminary. Though not one to make demands and elbow her way through, Marie Mathis, like other strong WMU presidents before her, showed no timidity in dealing with the brethren. The same can be said for one of her successors, Christine Gregory, who became, in 1981, the first woman ever to be elected first vice-president of the SBC. Gregory's ascendancy would mark the zenith of Southern Baptist women's upward climb in the SBC, for already the fundamentalist element in the denomination had elected two presidents and would continue electing them until, by 1991, they would have a strangle hold on the convention. With the fundamentalists' rise to power, the fortunes of Southern Baptist women would go into reverse. Not totally impervious yet to pleadings for the representation of women on important committees, the fundamentalist leadership placed Gregory and one other woman on the Peace Committee, appointed in 1985 to settle differences between the convention's fundamentalists and moderates. Gregory and other moderates on the committee had little impact upon the committee's report. The fundamentalists tightened their control, and over the next few years women would be put in their "proper sphere"—again.[49]

Alongside the strong presidents who led the WMU were the able women who usually ran the WMU. As indicated earlier, they used different titles at different times in the history of the

---

[49] Ibid., 105, 109–11, 113, 140–41; David T. Morgan, *The New Crusades, the New Holy Land: Conflict in the Southern Baptist Convention, 1969–1991* (Tuscaloosa and London: University of Alabama Press, 1996) 81, 86–88.

organization, but functioned as the executive officer. Annie Armstrong was a strong woman when dealing with women, but she was ordinarily subservient in her dealings with men. She firmly believed that Southern Baptist women should "stay in traditional feminine confines." Although she refused to speak at meetings where men were present, it should not be taken away from this influential woman that she did insist upon the establishment of the WMU in the face of male opposition and the hemming and hawing of her more timid sisters. Also, for eighteen years she directed the work of the WMU, in spite of conflicts with forceful women like Fannie Heck. Finally, her fame as a Southern Baptist is overshadowed only by Lottie Moon. She was a strong leader, and she prepared the way for other impressive executives like Kathleen Mallory, Alma Hunt, Carolyn Weatherford, and Dellana O'Brien.[50]

Kathleen Mallory served longer as WMU's chief executive than any other woman. She carried the title corresponding/ executive secretary from 1912 to 1948. As Armstrong did, she tended to defer to male leaders, and she was as totally dedicated to her work with the WMU as her more famous predecessor had been. She lived frugally in a single room and never owned an automobile. Unfortunately, as an Alabamian who grew up in the Jim Crow South, she constantly struggled to overcome her ingrained racial prejudice.[51] Though not bold in pushing for women's rights, Mallory did go beyond Armstrong's refusal to speak before men and led the WMU at a time when the organization received some significant concessions from the convention—namely, giving women more representation on committees and allowing women to address the conventions.

Alma Hunt, who was Mallory's successor as executive secretary (1948–1974), also sought and won concessions for

---

[50] Allen, *Laborers Together with God*, 164–67, 170–71.
[51] Ibid., 128, 182, 185–86, 189, 191.

Southern Baptist women, but she did it through compromise and not assertiveness. It is easily arguable that Hunt capitulated instead of cooperated with the denomination, for she allowed the Carver School of Missions and Social Work at Southern Seminary to be taken over by the SBC, the Royal Ambassadors to be transferred from the WMU to the Convention's Brotherhood Commission, and the management of WMU's mission funds to be shifted to the mission boards. In return for these concessions, however, the WMU was allowed participation in the convention's long-range planning and church programming. Along with Marie Mathis, Hunt apparently believed that she gained from the denomination a more important voice in planning its future, and she, with Mathis's help, reorganized the WMU to deal with the changing roles of women. Whatever the design of these two women, the WMU flourished under their leadership. Membership increased to over a million, and the Lottie Moon Christmas Offering climbed to unprecedented heights. Then came the period of 1964 to 1974, when racial unrest and the Women's Liberation movement stirred the nation's emotions, raising them to fever pitch. Although the WMU did not beat a drum for Women's Liberation or demonstrate for racial justice, the organization apparently suffered from the fallout that came from the upheaval those movements caused. Membership declined, there was a serious dip in the circulation of *Royal Service,* and the WMU budget was finally touched by red ink. Hunt announced her retirement.[52]

The departure in 1974 of Alma Hunt as the chief executive officer of the WMU saw that office filled, under the new label of executive director, by Carolyn Weatherford. Born in Mississippi and reared in Florida, this dynamic woman turned the WMU around. She asserted that women should do whatever was necessary to promote missions, and she spoke often and directly

---

[52] Ibid., 204; Fletcher, *The Southern Baptist Convention,* 205.

in favor of women's leadership. So impressive and so effective
was she that no one took her lightly, not even the brethren. In
spite of her views, she worked well with the male leaders of the
SBC. Her list of honors and achievements is long: the first
woman to chair the North American Baptist Fellowship; the first
woman to hold a chair of any Southern Baptist seminary's
alumni association; recipient of the New Orleans Baptist
Theological Seminary's Distinguished Alumnus Award in 1975;
and holder of five honorary doctor's degrees, all from Baptist
colleges and universities. For fifteen years, 1974–1989,
Weatherford promoted women's causes, including the new
women in ministry movement, and she resisted fundamentalist
pressure, beginning in the early 1980s, to make the WMU
subservient to the denomination. Before leaving office in 1989
she married, becoming Carolyn Weatherford Crumpler. Rejecting
fundamentalist views, Crumpler, having left the WMU, ran for
first vice-president of the SBC in 1989, as a sort of running mate
of moderate presidential candidate Dan Vestal. They went down
to defeat.[53]

Crumpler's successor in 1989 was Dellana O'Brien, and she
was cut from the same cloth as her immediate predecessor. She
was not to be pushed around by the fundamentalist leaders who
were now virtually dominant in the convention and who would
soon have complete control. Instead of pulling out of the
denomination, outnumbered moderates began to organize splinter
groups within it. One of the largest of them, the Cooperative
Baptist Fellowship (CBF), came up with an alternative funding
apparatus, designed to circumvent the Cooperative Program by
denying funds to SBC agencies under fundamentalist control.
Indeed, the CBF developed its own missions program and
encouraged churches that supported the CBF to send their money

---

[53] Allen, *Laborers Together with God*, 216, 219; Fletcher, *The Southern
Baptist Convention*, 301; Morgan, *The New Crusades, the New Holy Land*, 87,
101, 103, 125, 127.

for the support of that program. The WMU, under O'Brien's leadership, lent its approval to the alternative funding plan and, at the same time, tried to maintain ties with the SBC. Accused of getting involved in the controversy on the moderate side, O'Brien denied it and expressed regret for any appearance of such involvement. Despite O'Brien's denials, the WMU's attempt to straddle the fence in the controversy was viewed by fundamentalists as an endorsement of the moderate cause. Until health problems prompted O'Brien to leave her position in 1999, she was constantly confronted with criticism and pressure from the fundamentalist leaders of the SBC. Well before then she said that the WMU could no longer remain silent in the controversy, because that upheaval had a negative impact upon missions. "It's not WMU's fault that the controversy has changed our convention," she declared.[54] After a lengthy search for her replacement, O'Brien was succeeded in 2000 by Wanda Lee, who faced the monumental task of trying to keep the WMU true to its original mission of helping promote Southern Baptist mission efforts (fundamentalist and moderate) while remaining auxiliary to the Southern Baptist Convention.

Lee gave every appearance of being a worthy successor to the able WMU executives who had preceded her. An attractive, dedicated, and sincere woman, she was obviously totally committed to the organization and its mission. In an interview she told the writer that the WMU was all about missions at the outset, and it still was. For more than a quarter of a century, this nurse, by training, came through the ranks of the organization, serving in many offices—from Acteen sponsor to national president—before becoming executive director. She exuded confidence and was firmly convinced that the WMU remained on the right track in carrying out its mission. While she admitted that the relationship between her organization and the SBC was

---

[54] Ibid., 172–73, 188.

not what it had once been, she said that she had encountered no hostility from denominational leaders. On the other hand, she readily acknowledged that she had had no dialogue with them either. She had been told by the denomination's mission board presidents that the WMU was one of the SBC's "many partners." Operating from a budget of about fourteen million dollars in the year 2000—most of that money brought in from the organization's numerous publications—Lee seemed convinced that the future of the WMU was bright and that it would fulfill its mission, regardless of what the SBC did. Her bearing and manner suggested the strong, silent type, not one to engage in intense confrontation, but one who would quietly and firmly state her position and not be intimidated into changing it. As far as controlling the WMU, the SBC leadership had apparently given up on that idea and with good reason, according to Lee.[55]

Given the history of the WMU, its accomplishments are simply amazing. If nothing else were considered but the Lottie Moon Christmas Offering and the Annie Armstrong Easter Offering, both of which have raised astronomical amounts for foreign and home missions, the WMU would have to be judged as one of the most effective religious organizations ever established. Its contributions are legion. Amazingly, only a small percentage of the money raised through the WMU has gone to administer its operation through the years—never more than 5 percent a year. All the rest has gone to missions and the WMU's educational and charitable activities. The big question is: Why did the women persist in doing so much for a denomination that did not even give the WMU a place in the SBC constitution and bylaws until 1959, when it was *mentioned* in a bylaw "as an auxiliary of the convention"? Moreover, the women who created the WMU and carried it on from its beginning until the year 2000 have often been under-appreciated and even criticized for wanting nothing

---

[55] Author's interview with Wanda Lee, March 1, 2001.

but to do good in the name of God. They had to fight for acceptance for years after their organization was founded, with male leaders in some states trying to prevent establishment, and at least in one instance, asking a thriving state WMU to disband. In 1916, when the Sunday School Board undertook to publish the *Methods Manual* for the purpose of delineating church operating methods, the manual's author, S. E. Tull, objected to Kathleen Mallory's insistence that women in local churches should receive credit for their contributions. Tull argued that such organizations as the WMU should never have been fundraising groups in the first place and insisted that their purpose was educational only. Some male critics challenged the preamble to the WMU constitution, claiming that instead of saying "We the women of the churches," it should read "We the handful of the women."

The worst of the criticism died down after the 1920s, but it surfaced again with perhaps even greater hostility when the WMU started promoting women in church-related vocations during the 1970s. The negativism was never as bitter, except in the days of J. W. Porter, as it was in the 1990s, when the WMU ran afoul of the new fundamentalist leaders of the SBC. The organization came under heavy attack from the likes of Adrian Rogers, the fundamentalist president who began an unbroken line of presidents of his stripe with his election in 1979. In 1993 he claimed that "woman's auxiliary should be hardwired into the denomination's structure," and he called for an end to the "feminization of missions." He called for the WMU's governing body to be elected by the messengers at the SBC's annual meetings. In 1995 a committee charged with restructuring SBC agencies drafted a proposal that stripped from the WMU its responsibilities for promoting missions and education in the SBC. The proposal was passed at the Atlanta convention that year, but with an amendment "affirming WMU." Dellana O'Brien did not view the amendment as much of an affirmation of her organization, declaring that the SBC was a male-dominated denomination that had always rejected leadership roles for women. Thus, she reinforced Carolyn Weatherford's observation: "If women had leadership roles outside Woman's Missionary Union, history is silent." In the face of charges that the WMU was a liberal, feminist organization, O'Brien denied that this was true, except, perhaps, in the case of a mere handful of members. Not only were the fundamentalists hurling barbs, they were busy organizing their own women's ministry at the Sunday School Board. There were even attempts to charge the WMU for its meeting-hall expenses for the 1992 SBC annual meeting.[56] The fundamentalists made it quite clear through the 1990s where the WMU stood in their opinions, and it was at a point not too far above sea level! In Wanda Lee's mind, the hostility that was so apparent in the mid-1990s toward the WMU had turned to resignation by the time she took the reins of the organization.[57]

From the very beginning the WMU had to bear the criticisms and opposition of Southern Baptist male chauvinists. For 112 years that sentiment always lurked beneath the surface of Baptist life, although there were periods when women were more tolerated and accommodated than they were at other times. Because there were always some fair-minded Southern Baptist men who supported the rights of women, the WMU had a glimmer of hope that the organization's status would gradually improve until one day women would be regarded as equal to men. Then their organization would be appropriately appreciated by the denomination for which they had done so much. Their longsuffering did not pay off, however. They waited in vain

---

[56] Allen, *A Century to Celebrate*, 47, 53–54, 69–70, 96–97, 293, 343; Editorial, *Baptists Today*, 9 November 1995, 5, 10; Fletcher, *The Southern Baptist Convention*, 331–32, 343–45, 379; Carolyn Weatherford, "Shaping of Leadership Among Southern Baptist Women," *Baptist History & Heritage* (July 1987) 15.

[57] Author's Interview with Wanda Lee, March 1, 2001.

because the modest progress that was made for sixty years from about 1920 to 1980 ended abruptly when Southern Baptist fundamentalists captured the denominational reins of power. In the year 2000 the Woman's Missionary Union, Auxiliary to the Southern Baptist Convention, had become, in Wanda Lee's words, one of the SBC's "many partners," and the WMU had become more "church-focused" than "denominational-focused." Meanwhile, the SBC had started its own "Women's Enrichment Ministry," which sponsored rallies and Bible studies led by a woman from Texas named Beth Moore. By all appearances, at the beginning of the twenty-first century, the denomination was relying on the WMU far less than in the past, and the WMU was moving forward, doggedly determined to carry out its mission on its own, supported by its million members and its substantial budget.[58]

---

[58] Ibid.

CHAPTER 6

"BUT I KNOW I WAS CALLED"

THE QUEST OF SOUTHERN BAPTIST WOMEN FOR ORDINATION

In the year 2000, at their annual convention in Orlando, Florida, Southern Baptist messengers took a very strong stand against women being ordained and becoming pastors of Southern Baptist churches. This action did not faze eleven Virginia churches that had women pastors. Carol Johnson, the senior pastor of Troutville Baptist Church, reacted by saying, "When people mention Timothy [1 Tim 2:11-12], I think 'But I know I was called.'" Johnson went on to say that she kept remembering that God chose Deborah in the Old Testament to be a judge over the nation of Israel and concluded, "God can choose anyone, whether it's male or female."[1]

Because of the decentralized nature of Baptist church polity, the local church can do as it pleases, even to the point of totally ignoring the declared stance of associations, state conventions, and the SBC. This can lead, of course, to one or more of the

---

[1] *Religious Herald*, 15 June 2000, 3–4.

Baptist bodies withdrawing fellowship from a church that is deemed out of line. That is what happened in the Sehested case when the Shelby Baptist Association withdrew fellowship from the church she pastored. It happened in some other cases, as well. As indicated earlier, the year 2000 found Sehested out of the pastoral ministry and serving as a prison chaplain in North Carolina. Many other women have defected to other denominations, while a number have remained in Southern Baptist churches that have chosen to remain in the denomination while asserting their autonomy in defiance of the SBC's banning women pastors at the 2000 convention in Orlando. It remains to be seen if such churches can live at peace and be comfortable in a denomination, now controlled by fundamentalists for a decade or more, that has forbidden women to be ordained to the pastoral ministry.

The action taken against women at the 2000 annual convention represents a decades-old struggle among Southern Baptists that has now ended in defeat for women and victory for fundamentalists and other male chauvinists in the SBC. From the outset most Southern Baptist men wanted to exclude women from the pulpit and the deacons' meeting. That could be done by refusing to ordain women, since both pastors and deacons are ordained as a prelude to serving in their respective offices. In all fairness to the brothers of the SBC, it must not be forgotten that all of this was generally true of other mainline Protestant churches until after World War II. It should also be remembered that there have always been exceptions to the rule in the various churches, ever since the Protestant Reformation. Leadership roles, or mostly the lack of leadership roles, of women in the churches has already been touched upon. Still, the ordination of women *per se* has not been examined specifically, and it needs to be. Leadership and ordination go hand in hand, but women have long exercised leadership without—in the vast majority of cases, at least—being ordained. In seeking ordination as deacons and pastors during the last half of the twentieth century, women have sought to carry their leadership to a new and higher level and, indeed, to legitimize it. Since Southern Baptists, and other Protestants as well, ordain deacons and ministers, it is necessary to examine the record of women being ordained to both offices.

Blanket statements about the role of women, whether the discussion is about ordination or simply playing a prominent role in the church, are just not appropriate. The record is mixed. With that in mind, an attempt will be made first to reveal the story of women deacons, or deaconesses, and second the history of women ministers. At the outset it should be made clear that there are examples of women deacons in Baptist history from the beginning to now, but one must search diligently to find them. Modern-day Baptists trace their lineage back to the earliest English Baptists of the seventeenth century. Among those first English Baptist leaders were John Smyth and Thomas Helwys. In 1609 Smyth said that "the Church hath powre to Elect, approve & ordeyne her own Elders, also: to elect, approve & ordeyne her own Deacons both men & women." Two years later, Helwys said, "That the Officers off everie Church or congregation are either Elders who by their office do especially feed the flock concerning their soules...or Deacons Men and Women who by their office releave the necessities off the poore." One critic of the English Baptists ridiculed them as consisting of "Trades-men & mostly women." Thus it appears that women played an important role among Baptists in the beginning, but that changed with the passage of time. Little by little women were assigned to lesser roles, and by the mid-nineteenth century many churches had abolished the office of deaconess, and some questioned the right of women even to vote on church matters.[2]

---

[2] Jann Aldredge Clanton, "Why I Believe Southern Baptist Churches Should Ordain Women," *Baptist History & Heritage*, XXIII (July 1988) 52–54; Christine Leigh Heyrman, *Southern Cross: The Beginnings of the Bible Belt*

Surprisingly, in colonial America Baptist women enjoyed their most active roles in the South, particularly among the Separate Baptists who had sprung from the Great Awakening and had migrated to the Southern back country from New England. Separate Baptist women were ordained as deaconesses and sometimes as "eldresses." There were even women preachers among them, including Martha Stearns Marshall, the wife of Daniel Marshall and the sister of Shubal Stearns. Stearns led the Separate Baptists in founding the Sandy Creek Baptist Church and the Sandy Creek Association in the mid-1750s, and his sister Martha was said to be able to reduce audiences to tears with her "prayers and exhortations."[3]

Such activities were met with mixed feelings by Regular Baptists like Morgan Edwards, who was pastor of Philadelphia's First Baptist Church. In the 1760s and 1770s he toured the South and noted in his reports that the work of the eldress "consists in praying, and teaching in their separate assemblies...consulting with sisters about matters of the church which concern them and representing their sense thereof to the elders; attending at the unction of sick sisters, and at the baptism of women, that all may be done orderly." Edwards made it clear that he disapproved of women speaking or governing.[4] Perhaps Separate Baptist women confined their activities to working with other women, as the Philadelphia pastor suggested, but that is not what some of the records indicate. It is altogether possible that Edwards knew that Separate Baptist women were more involved in church affairs than he indicated and just did not want his fellow Regular Baptists to reject the Separates out of hand, for many Regular Baptists

---

(New York: Alfred A. Knopf, 1997) 303 n.10 and 304 n.10; Leon McBeth, *Women in Baptist Life* (Nashville: Broadman Press, 1979) 29, 34, 37.

[3] Clanton, "Why I Believe Southern Baptist Churches Should Ordain Women," 53–54.

[4] McBeth, *Women in Baptist Life*, 39.

were already critical of their Separate brethren because they allowed too much participation by women.

Once the various Baptist groups united after the American Revolution, Baptist women became less and less equal in the affairs of their churches. Still, there were churches that had deaconesses. They were just few in number. A year after the Southern Baptist Convention was founded in 1845, R. B. C. Howell, who was a founder and leading architect of the denomination, published a book called *The Deaconship, Its Nature, Qualifications, Relations, and Duties.* He concluded that deaconesses were scriptural and were "as necessary as they were in the days of the apostles." Their purpose, however, was to help deacons in ministering to women, and they were not to be ordained. Hence, some churches continued having deaconesses, but there were far more churches that did not have them.[5]

At the end of the Civil War one daring man proposed that Baptist churches use women's talents in churches and disregard Paul's restrictions against doing so. That bold man was Samuel Boykin, editor of the *Christian Index.* In an editorial in 1865 he argued that Paul's views were reflections of first-century culture and nothing more. Boykin called for a more active role for Baptist women. Six years later an article in the *Religious Herald* recommended that Virginia Baptist churches have two women deaconesses on the church payroll to minister to women and families and to teach women the Bible.[6]

At all times, from the very outset, there were churches scattered throughout the SBC that had deaconesses. In 1874 the minutes of the First Baptist Church of Raleigh, North Carolina, stated, "On Friday, August 21, 1874 Bro Pritchard [the pastor] gives notice he shall insist on electing deaconesses. Motion to adjourn prevails." Just over two weeks later, four

---

[5] Ibid., 20, 140.
[6] Ibid., 141–42.

deaconess—sisters Sallie Towler, Mrs. A. M. Lewis, Mrs. V. B. Swepson, and Ana Justice—were elected. In faraway Waco, Texas, during 1877 the First Baptist Church of that city elected six deaconesses. The Third Baptist Church of St. Louis had a long history of electing deaconesses. After 1880 there was less discussion of deaconesses. Apparently the office went into something of an eclipse after deacons came to be regarded not so much as ministers but as managers of the church who assisted the pastor with the poor and needy. However, First Baptist Church of Raleigh continued its practice of utilizing the talents of women. On 5 December 1896 the church's finance committee had an equal number of men and women. In 1925 the church had twenty-four men and twelve women serving as deacons and deaconesses respectively, but until 1941 the deaconesses were not ordained. In 1962 sixteen women served and forty-four men, but by 1986 there were only thirty-two men serving alongside sixteen women. Meanwhile, in 1978 two women were nominated to be vice-chairmen of deacons, and Jane Purser was elected. That same year women began taking the offering and serving communion. Then, in 1980, a woman named Caralie Brown was elected chairperson of deacons. Scattered about the SBC were other churches like First Baptist of Raleigh that had women deacons, as deaconesses came to be called. For instance, there was Wake Forest Baptist Church in North Carolina and Danville Baptist Church in Georgia. The latter church actually ordained a woman deacon in 1931.[7]

During the 1970s there was a major shift in point of view regarding the advisability of ordaining women as deacons. A variety of voices began to be heard advocating a drastic change in

---

[7] Caralie N. Brown and Jane Purser, "Deaconesses: A Long History of Service," Baptist History Files, Women Deacons, Southern Baptist Historical Library and Archives, Nashville, TN, 1–3, 5–8, 10; McBeth, *Women in Baptist Life*, 143–44; Rufus Spain, *At Ease in Zion: A Social History of Southern Baptists, 1865–1900* (Nashville: Vanderbilt University Press, 1961) 169.

women's roles. In 1973 the student senate at Southern Seminary passed a resolution affirming the right of women to serve as deacons and to "interpret and answer the call to the Christian ministry, regardless of what form that ministry may take." Jean Wright of Watts Street Baptist Church in Durham, North Carolina was ordained as a deacon of that church in 1974, and two years later she was elected chairperson. In 1978 nine of the twenty-four active deacons at the Watts Street Church were women, some of whom had been ordained during the 1960s. As early as 1975 it was estimated that 200 to 300 Southern Baptist churches in ten states and Washington, DC had women deacons. By 1976 Baptist churches in Virginia had ordained more than 500 women deacons. Before the 1970s ended there were thousands of women deacons, mainly in Virginia, Kentucky, Texas, and North Carolina.[8]

The mounting number of women deacons in Southern Baptist churches was not appreciated by nor acceptable to the fundamentalists who were gradually laying hold to power in the SBC during the 1980s. Convinced that the Bible allows for only men to preach and have authority in the church, the fundamentalists were determined that the offices of pastor and deacon be occupied by men. When it came to light in 1983 that several churches in Oklahoma had ordained women deacons, there was an outcry against what fundamentalists regarded as a violation of scriptural teaching. Among the churches that came under condemnation were the First Baptist Churches of Norman, Oklahoma City, and Shawnee and Parkview Baptist Churches of Tulsa. The Capital Baptist Association was urged on by Bailey Smith, a former fundamentalist SBC president who had said that

---

[8] *Baptist Standard*, 24 October 1973, 4; Wayne Flynt, *Alabama Baptists: Southern Baptists in the Heart of Dixie* (Tuscaloosa and London: The University of Alabama Press, 1998) 536; Leon McBeth, "The Role of Women in Southern Baptist History," *Baptist History & Heritage* (January 1977): 22, 24; McBeth, *Women in Baptist Life*, 139.

God does not hear the prayer of a Jew. Oklahoma was not the only state where tension mounted over the issue. Churches were disfellowshiped by their associations in Alabama and Kentucky in 1987 for ordaining women as deacons.[9] As was the case in so many other matters, the denomination could not prevent any church from ordaining women because of local church autonomy, but churches found themselves frowned upon in some cases and ostracized in others when they did not strictly adhere to the new fundamentalist line on women's issues.

Ordaining women as deacons was unacceptable to fundamentalists and other biblical literalists because ordination symbolized a bestowal of authority and because, they believed, the scriptures forbade women to exercise authority over men. Their aversion to ordaining women as deacons, however, was not nearly as strong as the revulsion they experienced at the thought of ordaining women as pastors. Just as there was a long history of women deacons in the Christian church in general and in Baptist churches in particular, there was likewise such a history with regard to women preachers. One advocate of ordaining women to preach asserted in 1988, "God calls women to minister; there is no question about that." That writer, Carolyn DeArmond Blevins, went on to say that women have been ministering in the name of the Lord for centuries and named such Old Testament women leaders as Deborah, Miriam, and Huldah. While this contention is true, it is also true that women ministers, whether in ancient or modern times, have been the exception to the rule. It is clear that most Protestant denominations have discouraged women from occupying pulpits, and the list of women preachers in all denominations before the end of World War II is a short one. How many Anne Hutchinsons and Martha Marshalls were there in colonial America? It is difficult to find references to the

---

[9] David T. Morgan, *The New Crusades, the New Holy Land: Conflict in the Southern Baptist Convention, 1969–1991* (Tuscaloosa and London: University of Alabama Press, 1996) 155, 157.

relatively small number of women preachers, and the ones who can be found were usually not ordained. John Smyth might have approved of women deacons, but not women preachers. He said, "Women are not permitted to speak in the church in tyme of prophecy." Over a century later the brethren of the Philadelphia Baptist Association said that they would allow women to speak under certain circumstances, but they would not "open the floodgate of speech." It was stated plainly that women could not teach, govern, or lead.[10]

While a few bold women raised their voices on spiritual matters in both the seventeenth and eighteenth centuries, the right of women to preach became increasingly controversial and brought on a battle of sizeable proportions among all the Protestant churches during the nineteenth century. There were occasional compromises on the issue, but generally speaking the debate "continued into the twentieth century." Still, a goodly number of women did preach in the nineteenth century, and a few were even ordained. It was estimated that near the end of the nineteenth century 500 women had preached in Protestant pulpits and that at least "a score" were pastors. There is not a record of even one, however, being ordained in a Southern Baptist church. In fact, the refusal of Southern Baptists to ordain women continued for years. Between 1879 and 1920 the records show that there were about 150 Baptist women ministers. Again, not one of them was in the South. The nearest one to the South was in West Virginia.[11]

---

[10] Carolyn DeArmond Blevins, "Ordination of Women: Wrong or Right?" *The Theological Educator* 37 (Spring 1988) 100–101, 106; McBeth, *Women in Baptist Life*, 30–31, 37–39, 49–50, 58–61.

[11] "Findings: Baptist Women in Ministry, 1638–1920," Baptist History Files. Southern Baptist Historical Library and Archives, Nashville, TN. Susan Hill Lindley, *"You Have Stept Out of Your Place:" A History of Women and Religion in America* (Louisville: Westminster/John Knox Press, 1996) 118–28; McBeth, *Women in Baptist Life*, 49–50, 58–61; Rosemary R. Ruether

Generally speaking, the struggle to achieve the right for women to be ordained to the ministry went on in the vast majority of Protestant denominations with little progress until after World War II. Beginning in the 1950s one denomination after another began to recognize a woman's right to preach and be ordained,[12] but such was not the case in the SBC. Finally, in the 1970s Southern Baptist women asserted themselves and claimed the right to ordination and the pastorate. It is necessary now to look back and review the record of Southern Baptists in this matter, for doing so will shed light on the return, in the 1980s, to the policy of "women-must-stay-out-of-the-pulpit." In his history of the Southern Baptist Convention, published in 1954, W. W. Barnes made an astute observation. He wrote: "Southern Baptists, in particular, were ultra-conservative on the question of women taking any part in church life, especially in the matter of women speaking before mixed audiences.... Women's entrance into religious activities in public had to proceed a short step at a time."[13]

Conservative Southern Baptist men and not a few *Southern Baptist women* were terrified by the prospect of women mounting pulpits, in spite of the fact that such women as Martha Marshall, Margaret Meuse Clay, and Hannah Lee had been preachers among the Separate Baptists, who were forebears of Southern Baptists. Clay was even arrested in Virginia for

---

and Rosemary Skinner Keller, eds., *Women and Religion in America*, 3 vols. (San Francisco: Harper & Row, Publishers, 1981–1986) 1:205, 208.

[12] Harry N. Hollis, Jr. and others, *Christian Freedom for Women and Other Human Beings* (Nashville: Broadman Press, 1974) 24–25; Janet W. James, ed., *Women in American Religion* (Philadelphia: University of Pennsylvania Press, 1976) 13, 21–22, 171; Lindley, *"You Have Stept Out of Your Place,"* 311–12, 315–16, 391; Ruether and Keller, *Women and Religion in America*, 3:299; Elizabeth H. Verdisi, *In But Still Out: Women in the Church* (Philadelphia: Westminster Press, 1976) 34–35, 99, 106, 113–14, 134.

[13] William W. Barnes, *The Southern Baptist Convention, 1845–1953* (Nashville: Broadman Press, 1954) 140.

preaching without a license, not that it fazed her in the least. The merger of the Separates with other Baptists soon resulted in a sharp change in attitude. All through the nineteenth century Southern Baptists were firmly committed to the belief that women should not speak in mixed assemblies. One objection—by women as well as men, it will be remembered—to the founding of the Woman's Missionary Union Training School in 1907 was that it would turn women into preachers. Josiah W. Bailey, the editor of the *Biblical Recorder*, argued that "Our Seminary will prevent the young women from becoming preachers, granting that any of them should so far miss their aim." He went on to say that the training school would guarantee women orthodox training under the control of men and would provide a source of suitable wives for the men students. It was probably this attitude that led the denomination's seminaries to admit women on an equal basis with men early in the twentieth century. Even that did not happen without considerable male opposition.[14]

Until J. W. Porter came along, no Baptist spokesmen were more adamantly opposed to women preaching to men than the two Southern Baptist luminaries, John A. Broadus and B. H. Carroll. Broadus died in 1895 and Carroll in 1914. To the very last Broadus insisted that "women should not speak in mixed assemblies," and Carroll asserted that "a woman pastor is in flat contradiction of the apostolic teaching and is open rebellion against Christ our King and high treason against his sovereignty." The vote in favor of seating women as messengers by the 1918 convention of the SBC prompted J. W. Porter, then editor of the *Western Recorder,* to edit a volume called *Feminism.* The book, which was published in 1923, consisted of essays that argued against women being allowed to preach. Porter feared that the

---

[14] Betty A. DeBerg, *Ungodly Women: Gender and the First Wave of American Fundamentalism* (Minneapolis: Fortress Press, 1990) 79; Lindley, *"You Have Stept Out of Your Place,"* 43; McBeth, "The Role of Women in Southern Baptist History," 18; McBeth, *Women in Baptist Life*, 44.

action taken in 1918, which enhanced the role of women in the convention, would lead ultimately to women mounting the pulpit. The Kentucky editor argued that women were morally superior to men, stating, "Sacrifice is her joy and crown. Her religious superiority should be compensation enough for her divinely imposed limitations." Almost a voice crying in the wilderness on the issue was that of Professor W. O. Carver of Southern Seminary. He called for a greater role for women in the SBC, claiming that for the first time in human history Jesus Christ put men and women on a basis of equality.[15] While Carver stopped short of advocating the right of women to preach, his assertions of women's equality implied that women should be allowed to do anything men were allowed to do.

The hard line taken against women preachers by Broadus, Carroll, Porter, and many others was repeated more forcefully in 1941 by maverick Southern Baptist John R. Rice. Quoting Paul in Corinthians and Timothy, Rice insisted, "There were no women preachers, no women pastors nor evangelists nor Bible teachers, in the New Testament churches." Passages that imply the presence of women preachers in biblical days were explained away by Rice. He blamed the emergence of "multiplied sects with false doctrines of every kind" on women preachers and claimed they do far more harm than good. In a word, Rice saw women preachers as the ruination of the Christian faith, stating, "Feminism in the churches is a blight that has grieved God and made ineffectual His power and it has disillusioned the people and lost their confidence. I have no doubt that millions will go to Hell because of the unscriptural practice of women preachers."[16]

While women preachers were certainly not numerous in 1941, there were enough of them around to alarm male

---

[15] *Baptists Today*, 4 April 1996, 14.

[16] John R. Rice, *Bobbed Hair, Bossy Wives, and Women Preachers* (Wheaton IL: Sword of the Lord Publishers, 1941) 25, 40, 43, 48, 51, 56, 58–59.

chauvinists like Rice. The first woman on record to pastor a Southern Baptist church did not live in the South. Druecillar Fordham, a black woman, was ordained by the National Baptists in 1942. She became pastor of Christ Temple Baptist Church of Harlem in 1963. That church was received into the Metropolitan (Southern) Baptist Association in 1972. Most Southern Baptists, because Fordham was in faraway New York on the periphery of Southern Baptist territory, probably were not even aware of her or her church. By the time Fordham became a Southern Baptist minister, the barriers against ordaining women to the ministry were coming down almost everywhere but in the SBC. Presbyterians had yielded to the inevitable in 1956, as had the Methodists. In the late 1960s the Lutherans followed suit, and the Episcopalians in 1976. Meanwhile, the Disciples of Christ had been ordaining women since the 1920s, and Free Will and Northern Baptists had long ago pioneered in ordaining women among Baptists. Among the major Protestant denominations, the one to hold out the longest was, of course, the SBC.[17]

Since all Baptist churches are autonomous, there were individual churches that were willing to act in the matter of women's ordination without the good wishes of the denomination. One of those was Watts Street Baptist Church in Durham, North Carolina. In 1964, when the church ordained Addie Davis to the ministry, the pastor was Warren Carr, considered by many to be one of North Carolina's most liberal ministers. It will be remembered that Carr and his church had already provoked controversy by ordaining women deacons. Davis was the first woman on record to be ordained in a Southern Baptist church in the South. Over the next fifteen years approximately fifty more women were ordained in various churches, and by 1979 a few were serving as pastors. Beginning in

---

[17] McBeth, *Women in Baptist Life*, 63–67, 69, 72, 156.

1973 the ordination of women ministers became a major issue at the denomination's annual conventions.[18]

Long before the controversy arose over ordaining women to the ministry, women had served in many churches as youth ministers, ministers of education, and ministers of music, but without the benefit of ordination. Even in these different ministries, however, men were given preference, and the number of women attending seminaries in preparation for such ministries had been on the decline until the ordination controversy of the 1970s revived women's interest in entering church vocations. The revival of women's interest in serving in such capacities also intensified the controversy. At the 1978 Consultation on Women in Church-Related Vocations one participant insisted that "when Eve misbehaved in the Garden she showed that women have an inherent weakness that is built into womanhood." The man making this remark also accused the WMU of bringing the women's movement into the SBC by encroaching on male prerogatives in the church. In Alabama, where the WMU has its headquarters, there was strong opposition to ordaining women, even among women. A woman in the town of Columbiana called the Equal Rights Amendment and the bid for women to be preachers an attack on marriage and the church. Even so, there were some Alabama women and even men who endorsed women's ordination. The consensus of Alabama opinion was strongly against it, however. In 1970 Ruby Welsh Wilkins was licensed to preach by the Antioch Baptist Church of Wadley. The church was promptly tossed out of the Tallapoosa Baptist Association. No pastor would participate in Wilkins's ordination. For a while the Antioch Church prospered under her leadership, but eventually it became a point of controversy and ultimately split. Wilkins resigned as pastor in 1985. In the end she and her son became the only resident

---

[18] Ibid., 15–16.

members. In the meantime, in 1978, Grace Philpot Nelson, who worked as a chaplain, was ordained by the Mountain Brook Baptist Church. Nelson's husband, Dotson Nelson, was pastor of the church.[19]

Although one can find anomalies regarding women serving in Southern Baptist churches besides Addie Davis's ordination by Watts Street Baptist Church, her ordination remains the first dramatic departure from Southern Baptist tradition in the South, and it was the catalyst that led to an increasing number of Southern Baptist women determined to enter the pastoral ministry. Davis was no babe in the woods acting on impulse when she decided to seek ordination and become a pastor. She was a graduate of Covington High School in Covington, Virginia. Next she graduated from Meredith College in Raleigh, North Carolina. For a short time she served as Dean of Women at Alderson-Broadus College in Phillippi, West Virginia, before entering Southeastern Baptist Theological Seminary. When she requested ordination at Watts Street Church, Warren Carr and the entire congregation supported her wholeheartedly. Letters of complaint poured into the church from all over the SBC. Ordination was one thing; finding a church to pastor was another. Finding no pulpit open to her in the SBC, Davis became pastor of an American Baptist church in Readsboro, Vermont. In 1971 she was named "Minister of the Year" by the Vermont Baptist State Convention. After eight years she moved to another church in New England. Her admonition to Southern Baptist women was, "Don't give up if you have a call from God to enter the ministry."[20]

---

[19] Flynt, *Alabama Baptists*, 537–42; McBeth, "The Role of Women in Southern Baptist History," 18–19.

[20] Article clipped from *Called and Committed*, a publication by Southern Baptist Women in Ministry, Baptist History Files, Women in Ministry Group, Southern Baptist Historical Library and Archives, Nashville, TN.

Addie Davis's ordination threw open the door to women's ordination in Southern Baptist churches, but not immediately. Although there was a spontaneous outpouring of opposition as many Southern Baptists denounced Davis's ordination as unscriptural, the furor soon abated. After all, she headed north for Vermont, leaving the SBC far behind, and the autonomy of the Watts Street Church had to be respected. Also, her ordination was not soon followed by others. Actually it was seven more years—1971—before Shirley Carter became the second Southern Baptist woman to be ordained at Kathwood Baptist Church in Columbia, South Carolina. Carter was a chaplain at the state hospital, and she married W. Pringle Lee, a fellow chaplain and former Catholic priest. Just two months after her wedding, Carter announced that she was already pregnant when she married Lee and resigned her ministry "to save her and the church any future embarrassment." Apparently because of pressure from both the church and her employer, she forfeited her ordination and resigned her position as chaplain.[21] In all probability, this incident caused considerable comment to the effect that such could be expected when churches violated scriptural teaching by ordaining women to the ministry.

In spite of Shirley Carter's experience, the ordination of women continued. Soon after her ordination in Columbia, a Virginia church ordained Marjorie Lee Bailey, another chaplain. Bailey was the first woman on record to be ordained by a church affiliated with the Baptist General Association of Virginia. In 1973 came the ordination of Sue Fitzgerald, a native of Gretna, Virginia, who was ordained in North Carolina. Several women were ordained in Georgia in 1974. Two of them were Linda Jean Pruett and Hazel Grady, both ordained by Oakhurst Baptist Church in the Atlanta area. Grady, an associate minister of

---

[21] Baptist History Files. Women-Ordination. Southern Baptist Historical Library and Archives, Nashville, TN.

education, was a graduate of Mars Hill College and Meredith College and held a masters in religious education degree from Southern Seminary. The first woman to be ordained in Texas by a church affiliated with the Baptist General Convention of Texas was Jeanette Zachry. In 1974 she was ordained to the military chaplaincy ministry by Broadway Baptist Church of Fort Worth. The church's pastor was John Claypool. In presenting Zachry to the church for ordination, he said, "This girl is a chaplain at Lena Pope Home here and she has been accepted through our Home Mission Board to be an Air Force chaplain. Ordination is a prerequisite for acceptance." Thus did Broadway Baptist break new ground in Texas and ordain this twenty-four-year-old Southwestern Seminary student.[22] Accused of liberalism by many, Claypool was ultimately hounded from the SBC and became an Episcopal priest.

The trend toward ordaining women gained momentum in the mid-1970s, as other women were soon added to the list of those ordained as Southern Baptist preachers. The expanded list included Camile Adams, Octavia Applewhite, Susan Bishop, Claire Blackwell, Elizabeth Hutchins Boyle, Victoria Jean Brannon, Libby Bellinger Smith, Helen Lee Turner, and perhaps fifty others. In 1977 Marjorie Lee Bailey became senior chaplain of the Virginia State Penitentiary, the first female chaplain of any denomination in America to hold such a high appointment of that type. That same year Martha Gilmore was ordained by Cliff Temple Baptist Church of Dallas, the city's second largest Southern Baptist Church. Gilmore's ordination sparked a controversy when W. A. Criswell of First Baptist sharply

---

[22] Articles from the *Baptist and Reflector* and the *Baptist Standard,* Baptist History Files. Women-Ordination. Southern Baptist Historical Library and Archives, Nashville, TN.

criticized the Cliff Temple Church for what he regarded as committing an unscriptural act.[23]

The battle for or against women's ordination to the ministry was fought on many fronts in the SBC during the mid-1970s. After the 1974 annual meeting C. R Daley, editor of Kentucky's *Western Recorder*, noted with approval, "The convention refused to endorse or condemn the ordination of women but left it up to the local church, which is the way it ought to be." In Miami at the next convention, however, Christine Gregory of Virginia, newly elected WMU president, said women should be free to respond to God's call, whatever that call might be. If it were to be a pastor, that was between her and God. Even the president of the SBC, Jimmy Allen, endorsed equal rights for women in 1977 and urged Southern Baptists to give women more opportunities for service, apparently meaning more churches in which to serve as pastor. Meanwhile, in 1975 the District of Columbia Baptist Convention took a stand in favor of women's ordination. A study done in 1977 by Clay L. Price, an M.A. candidate at West Georgia College and an employee of the Home Mission Board, indicated that Southern Baptist attitudes on women's ordination were loosening up—at least a little. Among those who responded to a survey Price conducted, 17 percent favored women pastors, 24 percent favored ordaining women as chaplains, and over 75 percent favored ordination for women in the fields of religious education, youth ministries, or social work. Fifteen percent were open to calling a woman pastor, but only two respondents said that they would choose a woman over a man, if they were given such a choice.[24]

---

[23] McBeth, *Women in Baptist Life*, 153–58; Jesse C. Fletcher, *The Southern Baptist Convention: A Sesquicentennial History* (Nashville: Broadman & Holman Publishers, 1994) 225–26.

[24] Editorial comment from *Western Recorder*, Baptist History Files, Women's Role in Church, Southern Baptist Historical Library and Archives,

The proponents of a more liberal stance on women's ordination were quickly confronted by stiff opposition. In 1976 the Black River Baptist Association in Arkansas formally protested the ordination of women, saying its members would encourage "every church in our state" to remain true to the teachings of 1 Timothy 2:11-13. Then, at its convention in November 1977, the Arkansas Baptist Convention went on record "as looking with disfavor" on the HMB for "giving financial support to an ordained woman"—Susan Coyle. The Baptist General Convention of Oklahoma took a stand against women being ordained as ministers or deacons. A resolution was offered at the Kentucky Baptist Convention's annual meeting to preclude the ordination of women, but the wording was changed to leave the matter up to the local church. Similarly, at the 1978 meeting of the SBC, Mrs. Richard Sappington offered a motion against women being ordained, but her motion was ruled out of order. The rising tide of opposition to the ordination of women in 1977 and 1978 came as a reaction against Susan Coyle's ordination by her home church, Beech Fork Baptist in Gravel Switch, Kentucky, in February 1977. Coyle had a bachelor's degree from Centre College in Danville, Kentucky, and a Master of Divinity degree from Princeton Theological Seminary. A week after Coyle's ordination the executive board of the South District Association of Baptists of Kentucky asked its credentials committee to investigate. In April the board voted nineteen to nine to recommend that Beech Fork rescind the ordination or face ouster from the association. The church and its pastor, Mike Jamison, declined to honor the request. In October the association voted ninety-eight to sixty-four to withdraw fellowship, but the vote fell short of the necessary two-thirds vote required by *Robert's Rules of Order*. Coyle continued to be a

---

Nashville, TN; Fletcher, *The Southern Baptist Convention*, 293; McBeth, *The Baptist Heritage*, 692; McBeth, *Women in Baptist Life*, 135, 175.

controversial figure when the HMB offered to support her ministry. In the contentious atmosphere of the 1970s, when a Texas church pastored by Ralph Langley ordained Susan Sprague to the ministry, a pastor from California sent Langley a pair of pantyhose and a bottle of perfume that he asserted was appropriate for someone who had strayed so far from the teaching of scripture.[25]

In spite of the bitter opposition to women being ordained, some were not intimidated, and those brave souls moved steadily forward. Among them was Anne Rosser of Virginia. She and her husband Aubrey were called in 1979 as co-pastors of a church in Richmond. In 1980 Anne baptized three converts, presumably the first occasion in a Southern Baptist church where a woman pastor baptized anyone.[26]

As women pushed forward, insisting on their right to serve, some prominent Baptist pastors and leaders lent limited support. For instance, Duke McCall and Charles H. Ashcroft, highly respected academicians, along with Jimmy Allen, called for careful and thoughtful consideration of the matter of women's ordination, though they did not advocate it forthrightly. However, they came close enough to endorsing it to cause some to assert that they were advocates. With the fundamentalist effort to gain control of the convention, beginning at Houston in 1979, women's ordination increasingly became a hot-button issue. The women were determined to push for their rights, while fundamentalists were determined to stop them. At Charlotte, North Carolina, in October 1982 a meeting was held on issues affecting women. Nine of 150 women attending developed a rationale and plan for a support network. Nancy Sehested offered

---

[25] Carolyn DeArmond Blevins, "Patterns of Women Among Southern Baptist Women," *Baptist History & Heritage* (July 1987): 47; McBeth, *Women in Baptist Life*, 23–24, 159–62, 167–69.

[26] Fletcher, *The Southern Baptist Convention*, 292; McBeth, *The Baptist Heritage*, 691.

a report calling for national/regional conferences for women and for publishing a regular newsletter. Within weeks of this gathering a task force of nine men and women met at the SBC's Christian Life Commission (CLC) office to endorse and support this effort as a denominational venture. The CLC agreed to identify women in ministry as a special area of its work under a new woman staff member, Lela Hendrix. Carolyn Weatherford pledged the continued support of the WMU.[27]

In keeping with the WMU's promised support, the organization sponsored a Women in Ministry dinner on the eve of the SBC's annual meeting in New Orleans. On that occasion Sarah Frances Anders of Louisiana College presented a "white paper" on the status of women in ministry, calling for a network of support and fellowship. By this time there were at least 175 ordained clergywomen in the SBC.[28]

Significant steps forward were taken by the advocates of women's ordination in 1983. Nancy Sehested led the way in March of that year by enlisting thirty-three women to hold a conference to help open doors for women to minister and to name a preliminary task force. Those women met in Louisville and organized Southern Baptist Women in Ministry (SBWIM). Eight months later more than 200 women met at a session in Pittsburgh, just before the SBC met for its annual session. It was revealed at this organizational meeting of SBWIM that there were already 175 ordained "clergywomen" in the SBC and hundreds more waiting to be ordained. Soon after the bold step taken by Southern Baptist women to organize at Pittsburgh, Reba Cobb and Betty McGary Pearce organized a Women in Ministry Resource Center at Crescent Hill Baptist Church in Louisville,

---

[27] Paper by Carl L. Kell, "In the Name of Our Father and Mother: A Rhetorical Apologia for SBC Women in Ministry," Baptist History Files, Women in Ministry Group, Southern Baptist Historical Library and Archives, Nashville, TN, 3; McBeth, *Women in Baptist Life*, 170–71.

[28] Kell Paper, SBHLA, 1–2.

Kentucky, and began issuing a newsletter-type publication called *Folio*. Seven years later, in 1990, the Women's Resource Center and SBWIM merged, and in 1993 the organization dropped Southern Baptist from the name of their organization.[29]

Between the time that Southern Baptist women organized in 1983 and the time they removed Southern Baptist from their organization's name in 1993, there were ten stormy years of controversy, as alarmed fundamentalists in the SBC set out to thwart the movement for women's ordination. Brandishing 1 Timothy 2:11-12 they, along with other conservatives, insisted that women's ordination as pastors was unscriptural. Not to be caught unawares again, as they had been in Pittsburgh, the fundamentalists were ready on the women's issue at Kansas City in 1984. They sponsored a resolution encouraging the service of women "in all aspects of church life and work other than pastoral functions and leadership roles entailing ordination." The dubious rationale for that resolution was that women should submit to men because man was created first, and woman was first in the Edenic fall. Yet it passed by a vote of 4,793 to 3,466. Many in opposition to the resolution, including former SBC president Wayne Dehoney, insisted that it violated local church autonomy.[30]

Even before the stir over women in ministry at the Kansas City convention in 1984, there had been some trouble over the issue. On 12 March of that year a letter from the First Baptist Church of Midlothian, Illinois—a letter presumably written by the pastor—announced its withdrawal from the Chicago Metro

---

[29] Ibid., 3; "Opening Doors: A Brief History of Women in Ministry in Southern Baptist Life, 1868–1993," Baptist History Files. Women's Role in Church, Southern Baptist Historical Library and Archives, Nashville, TN; Fletcher, *The Southern Baptist Convention*, 271–72; Morgan, *The New Crusades, the New Holy Land*, 155.

[30] Fletcher, *The Southern Baptist Convention*, 271–72, 293; Morgan, *The New Crusades, the New Holy Land*, 156.

Baptist Association. The reason given was that on 13 February the association held a special business meeting to vote on withdrawing fellowship from Cornell Avenue Baptist Church "because they had violated scripture in calling a woman, Susan Wright, to be their pastor." The vote to disfellowship had failed to pass, and the association's failure to oust Cornell Baptist, according to the letter from First Baptist Midlothian, showed a "total disregard of scripture by the elected messengers." Therefore, First Baptist Midlothian had "no recourse but to remove ourselves from the fellowship of Chicago Metro Baptist Association." Furthermore, the letter warned, the church would pull out of the SBC, if the trend in calling women pastors continued.[31]

Susan Lockwood Wright, who was at the center of the controversy in Chicago, was fully qualified by her training to be the pastor of Cornell Avenue Baptist Church. She held a bachelor's degree from Georgetown College and a Master of Divinity degree from Southern Seminary, and she was not intimidated by her critics. At the SBWIM meeting in Kansas City a few months after the incident provoked by First Baptist Midlothian, Wright was one of the featured speakers. She said, "I bring you greetings from Cornell Baptist Church. The congregation wants you to know that they not only sent me joyfully to be with you this morning, but that they are also supporting us in prayer at this very time. Their desire is that this service bring honor to God and encouragement to women in ministry."[32]

Noting that she had been assailed from many sides, Wright indicated that she had received much support and that, despite being discouraged at times, she would follow God's lead. She said,

---

[31] Baptist History Files, Women-Ordination, SBHLA.

[32] "Proceedings of Southern Baptist Women in Ministry," Baptist History Files, Women in Ministry Group, Southern Baptist Historical Library and Archives, Nashville, TN, 9, 11.

"As I have sat through numerous meetings where brothers and sisters in Christ have denounced my ministry, rejected my call, and accused me of heresy or worse, I have often been discouraged—pushed to doubt and the brink of despair. The calls, the letters, and words of support have helped. But in the final analysis, it has to come down to whether or not I will follow Jesus Christ."[33]

Another speaker at the 1984 meeting was Lynda Weaver-Williams. She paid tribute to Wright and her church by calling them "the year's scapegoats," for "seeking to put feet to their faith and follow Jesus." Williams pointed out that women were doing great deeds of ministry as Southern Baptists, noting that a Southern Baptist woman in Virginia was the chaplain for a men's maximum security prison, that hunger-relief work in Louisville, Kentucky, was coordinated by a Southern Baptist woman, that for twenty years a dedicated woman had been minister of music at the First Baptist Church in a small Georgia town, and that the Christian social minister at Cooke County Hospital was a Southern Baptist woman. Elizabeth Barnes, an adjunct professor of theology and ethics at Southeastern Seminary, reinforced the observations of Williams, declaring the women present at the gathering as the "new womanhood called forward by God." Pointedly she said, "We are among those who are answering the divine Caller."[34]

For that significant meeting of SBWIM, 160 persons registered. It was estimated that 250 attended the Sunday morning worship service. Southern Baptist sisters were making it clear that they intended to heed God's call. Unfortunately, they learned a few days later, with the passage of the 1984 convention's resolution, that they would have to do it without the blessings of the SBC. The conservative and fundamentalist

---

[33] Ibid., 9.
[34] Ibid., 6–8.

elements in the convention were simply not going to have women in the pulpit or in any other office of authority. The fight was on, and it continued until the anti-women forces won the day less than a decade later. Individual churches might defy the wishes of the denomination by ordaining women and calling them as pastors—as a few did—but they would do so as mavericks in disagreement with the SBC's recorded stance.

Not only were women not wanted in the pulpit, they were not encouraged to serve as teachers in the denomination's seminaries either. In 1985 only 16.1 percent of students enrolled in 6 seminaries were women, while women made up only 2.2 percent of seminary faculty members, and only 3 women taught in schools of theology—Molly Marshall-Green and Pamela Acalise at Southern and Elizabeth Barnes at Southeastern.[35]

Women's interest in becoming ministers was growing, and in the minds of some, additional women in the pulpits of Southern Baptist churches was the wave of the future. In the summer of 1986 John E. Roberts, editor of the *Baptist Courier* (the journal of South Carolina Baptists) contended that the biggest change affecting churches in the previous two decades was the change in the status of women. He predicted that during the next two decades most Baptist churches would ordain women and that the number of women pastors—twenty-five to thirty at that time—would climb into the hundreds. At that juncture a report by the Center for Women in Ministry showed a list of 232 ordained Southern Baptist women, but it was estimated that there might be 75 more that were not known. A total of eighteen states had one or more ordained women, with North Carolina, Kentucky, and Virginia having the most. Yet, the most publicized incident involving a church's calling a woman pastor occurred in Tennessee, when Prescott Memorial Baptist Church of Memphis

---

[35] News Release by Wilmer C. Fields, Baptist History Files, Women in Ministry Group, Southern Baptist Historical Library and Archives, Nashville, TN.

tapped Nancy Sehested to lead that congregation in 1987. Mrs. Sehested became the first woman pastor of a Southern Baptist Church in Tennessee. A Texas woman whose father and grandfather were pastors before her, Sehested had been an associate pastor at Oakhurst Baptist Church in Decatur, Georgia. Her appointment by Prescott Memorial led to the church's expulsion from membership in the Shelby Baptist Association. Those who voted to expel Prescott Memorial contended that Eve's behavior in the Garden of Eden made women ineligible to lead congregations. Sehested's response was that people often used the Bible to support their "own biases and cultural prejudices." The following year, at the SBC's annual meeting in San Antonio, someone tried to nominate Sehested to preach the convention sermon in 1989. That person's motion was ruled out of order. The fundamentalist element was nearly in complete control of the convention by then, and women could forget about anything but opposition from the denomination's leaders when it came to matters of ordination and preaching.[36]

The more moderate among Southern Baptist men took refuge in the oft-heralded doctrine of local church autonomy. For example, Steve Tondera of Alabama, president of the Alabama Baptist Convention in 1986, said that the matter of women's ordination ought to be left up to each local church to decide. Tondera was apparently sympathetic to women's causes, for he stood in strong support of the WMU when the fundamentalists began to attack it. Moderates, though, like conservatives, came in different shades. One moderate group, which many Southern Baptists regarded as very liberal was the Southern Baptist Alliance. Among the moderates it had the fewest numbers, and it eventually changed its name to Alliance of Baptists. Even this group did not start out to champion a woman's right to serve as

---

[36] Fletcher, *The Southern Baptist Convention*, 272, 293; "Interview with John E. Roberts, editor of the *Baptist Courier*" *Folio* 4/1 (Summer 1986): 8–9; Morgan, *The New Crusades, the New Holy Land*, 156.

vigorously as some women expected. At one of its earliest meetings, held in Charlotte, North Carolina, on 1 and 2 December 1986 twenty-four people gathered. Four of them were women—two ordained and two not ordained. The ordained duo were Susan Lockwood and Nancy Sehested. When participant James Strickland suggested that helping churches that called women pastors would create good publicity for the group, Lockwood objected. She argued that the women's issue should not be used to make political hay. At the next meeting of the Alliance on 2 and 3 February 1987, Lockwood was elected vice president of the Alliance.[37]

The Alliance held its first "convocation" on 14 and 15 May 1987 at Meredith College in Raleigh, North Carolina. Former missionary Anne Neil was asked to chair a task force on women in ministry. When she later met with the Alliance Board, Neil was asked in "a not so friendly tone," "Just what is it you women want?" Pretty soon the feeling was expressed that the women were trying to take over the Alliance. There was some heated discussion as Neil pointed out that she had hoped the Alliance would be different from other "white male dominated" groups in Southern Baptist life. She asked if the Alliance intended to take women seriously and live up to its announced principles. Before the meeting ended, she was asked to serve on the organization's board and on the interim executive committee.[38]

Mrs. Neil was by no means through with shaking the tree of the fledgling organization then known as the Southern Baptist Alliance. In November 1987, at the Alliance's board meeting, she proposed that the organization give $15,000 for each of three years to employ a part-time person to serve as editor of *Folio* (SBWIM's journalistic organ) and coordinator for SBWIM. Some did not welcome the request. Nine years later, Neil wrote:

---

[37] *Baptists Today*, 4 April 1996, 14; Flynt, *Alabama Baptists*, 609.

[38] *Baptists Today*, 4 April 1996, 14–15.

"In what appeared to me to be a demeaning, condescending, patronizing gesture, the majority stated their wish to 'send a message of intent' by sending $1,000 from the mission fund. It was clear to me that the majority of the group was not yet ready to be supportive of Women in Ministry. I felt this action less than acceptable."[39]

Later, when the board appeared willing to give $5,000 to the newly formed American Association of University Professors' chapter at Southeastern Seminary, Neil reminded the members that they were only willing to give $1,000 to SBWIM. When someone asked if she could not see the blood of Southeastern faculty members flowing there on the floor, she responded, "Yes, I can; but can you see the avalanche of blood of women that has been flowing for nearly 2,000 years?" Silence engulfed the room, and Neil seriously considered abandoning the Alliance, but by January 1988 she came to detect "an almost palpable shift in attitude and spirit among us" and decided that there might be hope "for a partnership of equals." Neil soon went on to become the Alliance's third president.[40]

The creation of SBWIM and the support it finally got from the Alliance, which eventually increased its financial support fivefold to $5,000 annually, set in motion a rapidly increasing number of women's ordinations. Professor Sarah Frances Anders reported that the number of Southern Baptist women ordained to the ministry tripled between 1986 and 1992, rising to 900, which was still only 1 percent of the more than 90,000 ministers in the SBC. Still leading the way were the states of North Carolina, Kentucky, and Virginia. At that time there were only 18 women pastors, while about 200 women served as chaplains.[41]

As the number of ordained women increased, so did the opposition. In 1987 the Alabama Baptist Convention defeated a

---

[39] Ibid., 15.

[40] Ibid.; Morgan, *The New Crusades, the New Holy Land*, 83.

[41] Fletcher, *The Southern Baptist Convention*, 350.

resolution affirming women's role in the church by a vote of 788 to 644. Those in opposition voiced the concern that the resolution might be interpreted as endorsing the ordination of women. One student of Southern Baptist behavior during this period contended that "ordination has become Southern Baptists' weapon of choice," claiming that withholding ordination was the way Southern Baptists kept women from holding positions of leadership. By the early 1990s fundamentalists in the convention were attempting to block the appointments of prospective seminary faculty members who were open to women's ordination—even if those people held the "right" views on all other doctrines. Al Mohler, president of Southern Seminary, was a case in point. He noted that a stance against women pastors was required of new faculty there. "It's a hiring guideline. We hire only those that believe that," he said.[42]

The battle continued as the 1990s moved along. By 1993 there were over 1,000 Southern Baptist clergywomen, with 51 serving as pastors, 80 as associate pastors, over 200 as staff members, and more than 250 as chaplains. The number of women pastors climbed to 60 by 1995, and 176 women chaplains were endorsed by the HMB. It was estimated that about 10,000 Southern Baptist women performed ministerial work without the benefit of ordination. During 1993 there was an incident that demonstrated the unrelenting opposition of some Southern Baptist ministers to a woman holding forth in the pulpit. Citing 1 Timothy 2:11-13—of course—Wayne Keely, pastor of Faith Baptist Church in Claremore, Oklahoma, threatened to challenge the right of a woman to speak at the Oklahoma Conference on Evangelism. Under this pressure, the conference leader canceled

---

[42] Paper by Bentley, Baptist History Files, Women's Role in Church, Southern Baptist Historical Library and Archives, Nashville, TN, 4; Fletcher, *The Southern Baptist Convention*, 350; Flynt, *Alabama Baptists*, 586; Greg Garrison, "Baptists to Argue Women's Roles," *Birmingham News* (11 June 2000) 16A.

the speaking engagement of Ann Lotz, the daughter of Billy Graham. Keely argued that the Bible forbade any woman from ever speaking during church functions to men.[43]

Because of the attitude of Wayne Keely and others of his stripe, the decade of the 1990s witnessed the emergence of both despair and anger among Southern Baptist women who felt that God had given them gifts and called them to some sort of ministry. As the twentieth century ended and a new century dawned, Baptist Church of the Covenant in Birmingham, Alabama, called Sarah Jackson Shelton to serve as interim pastor. Mrs. Shelton, ordained in 1982 by Brookwood Baptist Church of Birmingham, had become somewhat disillusioned because of her failed efforts to find a pastoral niche among Southern Baptists. Her father, Lamar Jackson, had been a prominent pastor who had served Southside Baptist in Birmingham for many years until he retired about 1979. He was very supportive of his daughter's aspirations and was pleased when Brookwood Baptist decided to ordain her. Discussion over the women's issue was lively as Brookwood considered Shelton's request, but the church approved the ordination overwhelmingly. The event was not accompanied by altogether happy consequences, however. One young family and a single male left the church because of it. Then another woman staff member asked for ordination and received it amidst tension. Three years later the church exploded over the women's issue, and some months later the pastor left the church. In the years following, Shelton filled in here and there, preaching when asked, but mainly she spent her time attending to the needs of her husband and children. She was pleasantly surprised at the opportunity to be called as interim pastor by Baptist Church of the Covenant. She had given up attending the Alabama Baptist Convention, since she felt that

---

[43] Fletcher, *The Southern Baptist Convention*, 379; Sharon Leding Lawhon, "Women: Leading and Planning Worship," *Baptist History & Heritage* (July 1996): 52.

she was neither recognized nor accepted there. She took great pride in the fact that a homeless man who slept on the Church of the Covenant's premises told her that the word was "out on the street" that the woman preacher at the church was "preaching the word and laying it on them."[44] Thus, a gifted woman had gone her own way, alienated by the SBC and ignored by it.

Much the same can be said about two of Shelton's friends whom the author interviewed simultaneously with the interim pastor. One of them, Shirley Richards, was ordained the same year that Shelton was—1982. Richards saw her primary calling as pastoral counseling, which included preaching on occasion. She, like Shelton, had some disillusioning experiences in her quest to fulfill the ministry to which she was convinced that God had called her. As a student in the mid-1970s at Southwestern Seminary, she became frustrated and left the institution. In a pastoral ministry class the students were given an assignment to baptize two or three people in a group. When a male student could not believe that she had dared to carry out the assignment, she became angry and left the seminary. After much soul-searching she became convinced that it was biblical and right for her to pursue the ministry to which she was called and that meant seeking ordination, too, for ordination was a prerequisite of her employment as a pastoral counselor. She graduated from Southern Seminary in 1982 and was ordained by Crescent Hill Baptist Church of Louisville. Subsequently she got a Doctor of Ministry degree from Columbia Seminary in Georgia. She was working at the time of the interview with the Samaritan Counseling Center in Birmingham, an organization that retained only a limited connection with Southern Baptists. Dr. Richards freely admitted that she was totally disillusioned with the SBC. She still considered herself a Baptist, but not a Southern Baptist.

---

[44] Sarah Jackson Shelton, interview by David T. Morgan, Face to Face, Baptist Church of the Covenant, Birmingham, AL, 1 March 2001.

Having grown up a Southern Baptist, she had found it difficult psychologically to break her ties with the convention, but she said that she could no longer remain in a denomination that had veered so sharply from its traditional path.[45]

Along with Shelton and Richards, Denise Jacks, a Hospice chaplain and pastoral counselor in Birmingham, had some unhappy experiences with Southern Baptists in trying to win ordination and carry on her ministry. In the mid-1980s her church, Waller Baptist of Bossier City, Louisiana, gave its unanimous endorsement to her plans to attend Southwestern Seminary. After her graduation, however, the church refused to ordain her because "you are a woman." The letter that so informed her was written by the interim pastor, presumably after he had conferred with the church's deacons. Jacks had to wait until 1993 for ordination, when Baptist Church of the Covenant approved and ordained her. She had served ever since as a Hospice chaplain, but she noted that some people refused to be ministered to by her because of her gender—some of them Southern Baptists and some from other denominations.[46]

Women who aspired to ordination for the purpose of carrying on the ministry to which they believed God had called them were not the only ones who were becoming frustrated and angry over the "no-women-need-seek-ordination" policy of the SBC. As the twentieth century moved swiftly to its conclusion, at least one male pastor of a mega-church blasted the Orlando convention's action taken against the ordination of women. Hickory Grove Baptist Church of Charlotte, North Carolina, was supposedly the fifteenth largest church in the SBC. Its senior pastor, Joe Brown, was obviously agitated when he mounted the pulpit four days after the Orlando convention had added the

---

[45] Shirley Richards, interview by David T. Morgan, Face to Face, Baptist Church of the Covenant, Birmingham, AL, 1 March 2001.

[46] Denise Jacks, interview by David T. Morgan, Face to Face, Baptist Church of the Covenant, Birmingham, AL, 1 March 2001.

words "the office of pastor is limited to men as qualified by Scripture" to the Baptist Faith and Message Statement. The messengers had done so without a recorded single dissenting vote. Brown announced that the SBC "got him riled up" over its position on female pastors. A former Navy officer, Brown was married, the father of three children, and the senior pastor of a church with a ten-million-dollar annual budget. Upon looking at some facts about his church, one no doubt had to be puzzled about his sermon on this occasion. His church had twenty-one pastors and eighty-two deacons—all men. No doubt his congregation and Southern Baptists in general were shocked by his strident tone, as he heaped criticism on his denomination.[47]

Making his point with emphasis, Brown said:

> Now the Bible does not say for women to shut up.... The first people that heard about the resurrection were women. And the Bible says the angel of the Lord told the women to go and tell the men that Jesus had [been] resurrected. So, if the women had just shut up and not been a witness like the angel commanded them, we wouldn't be sitting here tonight.
>
> When the gospel was given, when Jesus gave the Great Commission, he didn't say, "Go you guys." He said, "Go ye." And you're not telling me there wasn't some ladies standing there.[48]

Continuing, Brown quoted 1 Timothy 2:12 and said that if Baptists were going to follow the part about women keeping silent, then they must also observe the surrounding passages requiring men to hold their hands in the air when they prayed and women to remove their gold and pearls. He told the men to put

---

[47] Ken Garfield, "Against the Baptist Tide," *The Charlotte Observer*, 11 September 2000, 1F, 4F.

[48] Ibid.

their hands in the air and women to remove their necklaces, even if crosses dangled from them. Uttering defiance, Brown declared that if a young woman came to his office and told him that she felt God was calling her to preach, he would tell her to "Go for it."[49]

When told of Brown's sermon, denominational official Richard Land emphasized that Brown was speaking as part of a minority. The fundamentalist leader noted that the people of the convention had spoken definitively on the issue, since only about thirty-five churches out of forty thousand had women pastors.[50] Land was doubtlessly correct in his observation, and that was the point. The vast majority of Southern Baptist churches, including many of their women members, did not want women in their pulpits. Still, there were hundreds of Southern Baptist women who felt a sense of God's calling to the ministry and thousands more Southern Baptists, women and a goodly number of men, who believed that the women who were called had every right to answer that call. Those who dissented from the official position that the denomination had taken in 1984, 1998, and 2000 faced the beginning of the new century with a decision to make. They could remain in the SBC, assert the doctrine of local church autonomy, and stand out as mavericks swimming against the denominational tide; or they could abandon the SBC, as Shirley Richards and many others did, and throw in their lot with another denomination. Even though the number of churches jumping from the convention ship was relatively small at century's end, more and more churches announced that they were severing their ties with the SBC, and in most every case the reason was the women's issue.

---

[49] Ibid.
[50] Ibid.

CONCLUSION

Women have not enjoyed equal status with men in the history of the Christian church in general or in Baptist churches in particular. Even so, attitudes toward women and their place in the church have fluctuated, being somewhat liberal at times among some groups and very conservative at other times. Catholics have been consistent through the centuries in assigning women a circumscribed role in religious affairs, while the many different Protestant groups have vacillated between the seemingly anti-woman views of the Apostle Paul and the more sympathetic position of men like the great evangelist George Whitefield. If one goes century by century, women were allowed to serve as deacons but not preachers by early English Baptists in the seventeenth century, and this practice continued deep into the eighteenth century. Surprisingly the American Revolution, which was supposed to be a great liberalizing force, led to women being relegated increasingly to an inferior status in most Protestant denominations. The nineteenth century proved to be a disaster as far as the advancement of women in the churches was concerned, especially in Southern Baptist churches.

Curtailing the rights and privileges of women during the first few decades of that century led women to rise up and demand their rights at the famous Seneca Falls Convention, held at Seneca Falls, New York, in 1848. A movement to promote the equality of women with men has been carried on ever since that famous gathering, though at times women have been more vocal and insistent than at other times. From 1848, off and on until the 1920s, women pushed hard for their rights and took a great step forward in the second decade of the twentieth century by winning the right to vote throughout the United States. In the 1960s and 1970s, after a long silence, women again pushed hard for total equality, only to come up short when the Equal Rights Amendment to the US Constitution narrowly missed ratification. As the twentieth century ended, women were still in search of total equality with men in American society.

Three years before the Seneca Falls Convention launched the movement for women's rights and equality in American life, Baptists of the South, intent upon preserving their legal right to own slaves, abandoned the Triennial Convention and established the Southern Baptist Convention. The attitude of Southern Baptists toward women at that juncture was essentially the same as the attitude of other American Protestant denominations toward women. Over time all of the denominations, including the SBC, gave some ground on women's issues, particularly just after World War I and soon after World War II. However, the SBC moved considerably slower than the others. The Women's Liberation movement of the 1960s and 1970s heightened awareness that women still occupied an inferior place both in society at large and in the churches, and militant voices among them began to make it clear that they were not going to take it anymore. Sadly, just about the time that some Southern Baptist denominational leaders were coming around to a more enlightened view, the SBC was taken over by fundamentalists in the years following the 1979 annual convention at Houston. The new leaders believed in biblical inerrancy and biblical literalism, and they were convinced that the Bible plainly taught that women should keep silent in the churches and occupy no places of authority. Not only did the fundamentalists believe these things, they institutionalized them in 1984, 1998, and 2000.

Thus, the SBC at the end of the twentieth century was obviously on a retrogressive path with regard to women's rights and equality.

One of the women historians who has spoken insightfully and at some length about the plight of Southern Baptist women is Carolyn DeArmond Blevins. As the twentieth century moved swiftly to its end, Blevins contributed an article titled "Reflections: Baptists and Women's Issues in the Twentieth Century." In that piece she asked all the right questions and brought forth some interesting answers to her own questions. "Do women really have a voice in Baptist life?" she queried. Her answer was that—at the end of the twentieth century—a Southern Baptist woman was "a strong soloist surrounded by a chorus of opposition."

Blevins discovered as she sought to answer this and other questions a number of interesting facts. For example, even on those rare occasions when women did speak before the SBC, as Ethlene Boone Cox did in 1929, the convention minutes failed to mention it. This caused Blevins to note, "Such omissions give evidence to the growing realization that often the contributions of women have been intentionally omitted from historical records." Blevins also observed that the state convention of Kentucky did not allow women to be messengers until 1956. Another glaring observation was made by Blevins: In 1999 half of the annual budgets of the International Mission Board (formerly Foreign Mission Board) and the North American Mission Board (formerly Home Mission Board) were met through the efforts of women, while women trustees on the two boards were outnumbered four to one. Moreover, with regard to the SBC's attitude toward the Woman's Missionary Union, which had contributed so much financially through the years to Southern Baptist missions, Blevins asserted that "convention forces are still at work eroding the independence and voice of the mission organization that has been the backbone of SBC missions for over a century." In the mind of this astute observer of Southern Baptist history and life, women have had no real voice in SBC affairs, and she is convinced that there was no small amount of hypocrisy attached to Baptist claims of commitment to the ideal of freedom. "We Baptists," she contends, "tout our doctrines of freedom while we muzzle our female voices."[1]

Women have traditionally enjoyed little status and virtually no voice in directing the destiny of the Southern Baptist Convention. In all fairness, however, it must be admitted that they were treated better during some time periods than others. Though obtaining some recognition during the suffrage movement and the years following the ratification of the Nineteenth Amendment, Southern Baptist women were fairly well ignored again during the 1930s and 1940s. When the Women's Liberation movement of the 1960s and 1970s once more focused the nation's attention on the inferior status of women, the more progressive brothers of the SBC became sympathetic to enhancing the status of the denomination's sisters. A small amount of progress was being made until Paul Pressler and Paige Patterson launched their so-called "conservative resurgence" at the end of the 1970s. That resulted in a fundamentalist takeover of the SBC and a return to women being assigned to their place, a place that did not include leadership roles in denominational affairs or ordination to the ministry.

All through those decades when Southern Baptist women were taking a step forward, then a step and sometimes two steps backward, and finally a long step backward into the nineteenth century, they were stubbornly finding their own vehicles for doing God's work. They persisted in going to the mission fields, often in the face of opposition, and many of them served with

---

[1] Carolyn DeArmond Blevins, "Reflections: Baptists and Women's Issues in the Twentieth Century," *Baptist History & Heritage* (Summer/Fall 2000): 54, 56–57, 65.

extraordinary distinction as both foreign and home missionaries. Southern Baptist sisters also went forward against determined opposition to establish their own organization in 1888—the Woman's Missionary Union. Except for missionaries like Lottie Moon and Willie Kelly, the Southern Baptist women who have acquired the most visibility and distinction have been the founders and leaders of the WMU—Annie Armstrong, Fannie Heck, Ethelene Boone Cox, Marie Mathis, Christine Gregory, Kathleen Mallory, Alma Hunt, Carolyn Weatherford Crumpler, Dellana O'Brien, Wanda Lee, and many others. After existing for 112 years the WMU could claim in the year 2000 a long list of noble contributions to a denomination that had reluctantly consented to its founding, that had intentionally sought to downplay its efforts, and finally had relegated it to the periphery of the convention as "one of many partners."

In the long run a telling commentary about the treatment of women in the Southern Baptist Convention might be that at the end of the twentieth century a former President of the United States, Jimmy Carter, along with his wife Rosalyn, renounced their membership as Southern Baptists. While the Carters did not cite the SBC's attitude toward women as their only reason for leaving the convention, it was clear that this was the catalyst that prompted them to depart. Jimmy Carter had served as a Sunday school teacher at Maranatha Baptist Church in Plains, Georgia, since he was eighteen years old, but he had had his fill of the "new" Southern Baptist Convention, a denomination that, in 2000, was firmly in the grasp of fundamentalists and male chauvinists. What the Carters no doubt saw was a denomination that was going full circle back to 1845, at least as far as its attitude toward women was concerned. Women had enjoyed no status in the Southern Baptist Convention when it had been founded at Augusta, Georgia, in 1845, and the Orlando convention of 2000 demonstrated that they enjoyed none as the twentieth century neared its end.

Sources Consulted

I. Primary

A. Baptist History Files in the Southern Baptist Historical Library and Archives

Harriet A. Baker

Women Deacons

Women Employees, SBC

Women in Ministry Group

Women—Ordination

Women's Role in Church, SBC

B. Official Records

Annual of the Southern Baptist Convention, 1845–2000

C. Contemporary Historical Studies and Commentaries

Broadus, John A. *Should Women Speak in Mixed Assemblies?* Louisville: Baptist Book Concern, Inc., 1904.

Heck, Fannie E. S. *In Royal Service: The Mission Work of Southern Baptist Women.* Richmond: Foreign Mission Board, 1913.

Hunt, Alma. *Reflections from Alma Hunt.* Birmingham: Woman's Missionary Union, 1987.

Porter, J. W., editor. *Feminism: Woman and Her Work.* Louisville: Baptist Book Concern, 1923.

D. Journals and Newspapers
Alabama Baptist
Baptist Program
Baptist Standard
Baptists Today
Biblical Recorder
Birmingham [Alabama] *News*
Birmingham [Alabama] *Post Herald*
Charlotte [North Carolina] *Observer*
Christian Index
Christianity Today
Folio
Religious Herald
Southern Baptist Missionary Journal
USA Today
Western Recorder

II. SECONDARY WORKS
A. Biographies, Histories, and Monographs
Allen, Catherine B. *A Century to Celebrate: History of Woman's Missionary Union.* Birmingham: Woman's Missionary Union, 1987.

———. *Laborers Together with God: 22 Great Women in Baptist Life.* Birmingham: Woman's Missionary Union, 1987.

———. *The New Lottie Moon Story.* Nashville: Broadman Press, 1980.

Anders, Sarah Frances. *Woman Alone: Confident and Creative.* Nashville: Broadman Press, 1976.

Banner, Lois W. *Women in Modern America: A Brief History.* New York and other cities: Harcourt, Brace, and Jovanovich, Inc., 1974.

Barnes, William Wright. *The Southern Baptist Convention, 1845–1953.* Nashville: Broadman Press, 1954.

Beaver, Robert Pierce. *American Protestant Women in World Mission: A History of the First Feminist Movement in North America.* Grand Rapids: William B. Eerdman's Publishing Co., 1968.

Blevins, Carolyn DeArmond. *Women in Christian History.* Macon GA: Mercer University Press, 1995.

Chafe, William Henry. *The American Woman: Her Changing Social, Economic, and Political Roles, 1920–1970.* New York: Oxford University Press, 1972.

Clark, Elizabeth Ann. *Women and Religion: A Feminist Source Book.* New York: Harper & Row, 1977.

Code, Joseph B. *Great American Foundresses.* Freeport NY: Books for Libraries Press, 1968.

Conway, Jill. *The Female Experience in Eighteenth and Nineteenth Century America: A Guide to the History of American Women.* New York and London: Garland Publishing Co., 1982.

Coon, Lynda and others. *That Gentle Strength: Historical Perspectives on Women in Christianity.* Charlottesville: University Press of Virginia, 1990.

Cott, Nancy F. *The Bonds of Womanhood.* New Haven: Yale University Press, 1977.

DeBerg, Betty A. *Ungodly Women: Gender and the First Wave of American Fundamentalism.* Macon: Mercer University Press, 2000 (Minneapolis: Fortress, 1990).

Douglas, Ann. *The Feminization of American Culture.* New York: Alfred A. Knopf, 1977.

Estep, William R. *Whole Gospel, Whole World: The Foreign Mission Board of the Southern Baptist Convention, 1845–1995.* Nashville: Broadman & Holman Publishers, 1995.

Fletcher, Jesse C. *The Southern Baptist Convention: A Sesquicentennial History.* Nashville: Broadman & Holman Publishers, 1994.

Flynt, Wayne. *Alabama Baptists: Southern Baptists in the Heart of Dixie.* Tuscaloosa and London: University of Alabama Press, 1998.

——— and Gerald W. Berkley. *Taking Christianity to China: Alabama Missionaries in the Middle Kingdom, 1850–1950.* Tuscaloosa and London: University of Alabama Press, 1997.

Fox-Genovese, Elizabeth. *Within the Plantation Household: Black and White Women of the Old South.* Chapel Hill: University of North Carolina Press, 1988.

Goldsmith, Barbara. *Other Powers: The Age of Suffrage, Spiritualism, and the Scandalous Victoria Woodhull.* New York: Alfred A. Knopf, 1998.

Graham, B. J. W., editor. *Baptist Biography.* 3 volumes. Atlanta: Index Printing Co. Publishers, 1920.

Greaves, Richard, editor. *Triumph over Silence: Women in Protestant History.* Westport CT and London: Greenwood Press, 1985.

Harkness, Georgia. *Women in Church and Society.* Nashville: Abingdon Press, 1972.

Hassey, Janette. *No Time for Silence: Evangelical Women in Public Ministry around the Turn of the Century.* Grand Rapids: Academie Books, 1986.

Hawks, Joanne V. and Sheila Skemp, editors. *Sex, Race, and the Role of Women in the South.* Jackson: University of Mississippi Press, 1983.

Hawley, John S., editor. *Fundamentalism and Gender.* New York: Oxford University Press, 1994.

Heyrman, Christine Leigh. *Southern Cross: The Beginnings of the Bible Belt.* New York: Alfred A. Knopf, 1997.

Hill, Patricia R. *The World Their Household: The American Woman's Foreign Mission Movement and Cultural Transformation, 1870–1920.* Ann Arbor: University of Michigan Press, 1985.

Hill, Samuel S. *Religion and the Solid South.* Nashville: Abingdon Press, 1972.

Hollis, Harry N., Jr. and others, editors. *Christian Freedom for Women and Other Human Beings.* Nashville: Broadman Press, 1974.

Hull, Gretchen. *Equal to Serve.* Tarrytown NY: Fleming H. Revel Company, 1973.

Hunt, Alma. *History of Woman's Missionary Union.* Nashville: Convention Press, 1964.

James, Janet Wilson, editor. *Women in American Religion.* Philadelphia: University of Pennsylvania, 1976.

Juster, Susan. *Disorderly Women: Sexual Politics and Evangelicalism in Revolutionary New England.* Ithaca: Cornell University Press, 1994.

Lindley, Susan Hill. *"You Have Stept Out of Your Place": A History of Women and Religion in America.* Louisville: Westminster John Knox Press, 1996.

McBeth, H. Leon, *The Baptist Heritage.* Nashville: Broadman Press, 1987.

————. *Women in Baptist Life.* Nashville: Broadman Press, 1979.

Montgomery, Helen Barrett. *Western Women in Eastern Lands.* New York: The Macmillan Company, 1910.

Morgan, David T. *The New Crusades, the New Holy Land: Conflict in the Southern Baptist Convention, 1969–1991.* Tuscaloosa and London: University of Alabama Press, 1996.

Olson, Jeanne E. *One Ministry, Many Roles: Deacons and Deaconesses through the Centuries.* St. Louis: Concordia Publishing House, 1992.

Porterfield, Amanda. *Feminine Spirituality in America.* Philadelphia: Temple University Press, 1980.

Rice, John R. *Bobbed Hair, Bossy Wives, and Women Preachers.* Wheaton IL: Sword of the Lord Publishers, 1941.

Rothman, Sheila M. *Woman's Proper Place: A History of Changing Ideals and Practices, 1870 to the Present.* New York: Basic Books, 1978.

Ruether, Rosemary R. and Rosemary Skinner Keller, editors. *Women and Religion in America.* 3 volumes. San Francisco: Harper & Row, Publishers, 1981–1986.

Scales, Laine. *All That Fits a Woman: Training Southern Baptist Women for Charity and Mission, 1907–1926.* Macon GA: Mercer University Press, 2000.

Scanzoni, Letha and Nancy Hardesty. *All We're Meant to Be: A Biblical Approach to Women's Liberation.* Waco TX: Word Books, 1974.

Scott, Anne Firor. *The Southern Lady: From Pedestal to Politics, 1830–1930.* Chicago and London: University of Chicago Press, 1970.

Sorrill, Bobbie. *Annie Armstrong: Dreamer in Action.* Nashville: Broadman Press, 1984.

Spain, Rufus. *At Ease in Zion: A Social History of Southern Baptists, 1865–1900.* Nashville: Vanderbilt University Press, 1961.

Spruill, Julia Cherry. *Women's Life and Work in the Southern Colonies.* Chapel Hill: University of North Carolina Press, 1938.

Starr, Edward C., compiler. *A Baptist Bibliography.* 25 volumes. Philadelphia: The Judson Press for the Samuel Colgate Baptist Historical Collection of Colgate University, 1947–1976.

Tucker, Ruth and Walter Liefield. *Daughters of the Church: Women in Ministry from New Testament Times to the Present.* Grand Rapids: Zondervan Publishing House, 1987.

Verdesi, Elizabeth. *In But Still Out: Women in the Church.* Philadelphia: Westminster Press, 1976.

Wyatt-Brown, Bertram. *Southern Honor: Ethics and Behavior in the Old South.* New York: Oxford University Press, 1982.

B. Articles

Anders, Sarah Frances. "The Role of Women in American Religion." *Southwestern Journal of Theology* 18 (Spring 1976): 51–61.

———. "The State of the Second Sex: Emancipation or Explosion?" *The Student* 53 (May 1974): 34–38.

———. "Woman's Role in the Southern Baptist Convention and Its Churches as Compared with Selected Other Denominations." *Review and Expositor* 72 (Winter 1975): 31–39.

Beck, Rosalie. "The Impact of Southern Baptist Women on Social Issues: Three Viewpoints." *Baptist History & Heritage* 22 (July 1987): 29–40.

———. "Texas Baptist Women Between the Wars: Invisible Women." *Texas Baptist History* 8 (1988): 10–17.

Blevins, Carolyn DeArmond. "Ordination of Women: Wrong or Right?" *The Theological Educator* 37 (Spring 1988): 100–11.

———. "Patterns of Women Among Southern Baptist Women." *Baptist History & Heritage* 22 (July 1987): 41–49.

———. "Reflections: Baptists and Women's Issues in the Twentieth Century." *Baptist History & Heritage* 35 (Summer/Fall 2000): 53–65.

———. "Women in Baptist History." *Review and Expositor* 83 (Winter 1986): 51–61.

Clanton, Jann Aldredge. "Why I Believe Southern Baptist Churches Should Ordain Women." *Baptist History & Heritage* 23 (July 1988): 50–55.

Cook, L. Katherine. "Texas Baptist Women and Missions, 1830–1900." *Texas Baptist History* 3 (1983): 31–46.

Elliot, Elizabeth. "Why I Oppose the Ordination of Women." *Christianity Today* (6 June 1975): 12–15.

Foss, Sara. "Flowing into the Mainstream." *Birmingham Post Herald*. 18 November 2000. 12D.

Garfield, Ken. "Against the Baptist Tide." *Charlotte Observer*. 11 September 2000. 1F, 4F.

Garrison, Greg. "Baptists to Argue Women's Roles." *Birmingham News*. 11 June 2000. 15A, 16A.

————. "New Leader Backs Proposal Against Women Ministers." *Birmingham News*. 14 June 2000. 1A, 2A.

Grossman, Cathy Lynn. "Great Baptist Schism Grows." *USA Today*. 12 June 2000. 1D, 2D.

Hinson, E. Glenn. "On the Election of Women as Deacons." *The Deacon* 3 (April 1973): 5.

————. "The Church: Liberator or Oppressor of Women?" *Review and Expositor* 72 (Winter 1975): 19–29.

Humphreys, Fisher. "Feminism and the Christian Faith." *The Theological Educator* 52 (Fall 1995): 15–20.

"Interview with John E. Roberts, Editor of the *Baptist Courier*." *Folio*. 4/1 (Summer 1986): 8–9.

Jewett, Paul. "Why I Favor the Ordination of Women." *Christianity Today* 19 (6 June 1975): 7–11.

Kaemmerling, Charlene. "Ordination of Women: Wrong or Right?" *The Theological Educator* 37 (Spring 1988): 93–99.

Lawhon, Sharon Leding. "Women: Leading and Planning Worship." *Baptist History & Heritage* 31 (July 1996): 48–58.

Letsinger, Norman H. "The Status of Women in the Southern Baptist Convention in Historical Perspective." *Baptist History & Heritage* 12 (January 1977): 37–44.

Lockett, Darby R."Feminist Footholds in Religion." *Foundations* 19 (March 1976): 33–39.

Lumpkin, William L. "The Role of Women in 18th Century Virginia Baptist Life." *Baptist History & Heritage* 8 (July 1973): 158–67.

Mann, Gerald E. "How We Got Women Deacons." *The Deacon* 5 (April 1975): 46.

Martin, Patricia S. "Keeping Silence: Texas Baptist Women's Role in Public Worship, 1800–1920." *Texas Baptist History* 3 (1983): 15–30.

————. "Ordained Work—Unordained Workers, Texas 'Bible Women,' 1800–1920." *Texas Baptist History* 8 (1988): 1–9.

McBeth, H. Leon. "The Changing Role of Women in Baptist History." *Southwestern Journal of Theology* 22 (Fall 1979): 84–96.

————. "Perspectives on Women in Baptist Life." *Baptist History & Heritage* 22 (July 1987): 4–11.

————. "The Role of Women in Southern Baptist History." *Baptist History & Heritage* 12 (January 1977): 1–25.

News Release. "Carter Breaks Ties with Southern Baptists." *Alabama Baptist* (2 November 2000): 4.

Pate, Billie. "Birth and Rebirth of Feminism: Responses of Church Women." *Review and Expositor* 72 (Winter 1975): 53–61.

Patterson, Dorothy Kelley. "Why I Believe Southern Baptist Churches Should Not Ordain Women." *Baptist History & Heritage* 23 (July 1988): 56–62.

Sisk, Ron. "Women in the SBC: A Status Report." *The Student* 64 (February 1985): 45.

Sorrill, Bobbie. "Southern Baptist Laywomen in Missions." *Baptist History & Heritage* 22 (July 1987): 21–28.

Stancil, Bill. "Divergent Views and Practices of Ordination Among Southern Baptists Since 1945." *Baptist History & Heritage* 23 (July 1988): 42–49.

Sumners, Bill. "Southern Baptist Women and Women's Right to Vote, 1910–1920." *Baptist History & Heritage* 12 (January 1977): 45–51.

Thompson, Evelyn W. "Southern Baptist Women as Writers and Editors." *Baptist History & Heritage* 23 (July 1987): 50–57.

Vickers, Gregory. "Models of Womanhood and the Early
    Woman's Missionary Union." *Baptist History & Heritage* 24
    (January 1989): 41–53.

————. "Southern Baptist Women and Social Concerns,
    1910–1929." *Baptist History & Heritage* 23 (October 1988):
    3–13.

Weatherford, Carolyn. "Shaping of Leadership Among Southern
    Baptist Women." *Baptist History & Heritage* 22 (July 1987):
    12–20.

Wyatt, Kristen. "Southern Baptists Too Rigid for Carters."
    Birmingham News. 21 October 2000. 1A, 4A.

INDEX